# AMAZON
# HITCHHIKER

## A Woman's Adventures from
## Canada to Brazil

## Alycin Hayes

ECHO HILL
PRODUCTIONS

Published by
Echo Hill Productions
Gainesville, Florida, USA
&
Harrington, Ontario, Canada
EchoHillProductions.com

Edited by Jacqui Corn-Uys

Cover design by Donika Mishinvea
www.aartofdonika.com

Photographs by Sergio Santos, Paulo Estevaletto, Suzanne Page,
JoAnn Hayes and Alycin Hayes

ISBN 978-0-9730320-4-8 (paperback)
ISBN 978-0-09730320-5-5 (ebook)

Library of Congress Control Number: 2021939892

## *Sister*

*Sister of the waves,*
*who sails by,*
*Saving images from*
*the teeth of indifference.*

*Who makes a friend*
*of distance itself.*
*The miles smile*
*back at her.*

*Even birds envy wings*
*such as hers;*
*for sailors cannot*
*catch her.*

*A dream, merely dreamed,*
*is a tear.*
*A dream realized,*
*is a diamond.*

*Sister of the waves,*
*a wealth of wisdom*
*will always be yours.*

*Jewels in your eyes.*

Poem by Elliott Hayes, for his sister, Alycin Hayes

## *Dedicated to:*

My wonderful, brave mother, who always had confidence in me and encouraged me to have the strength to chase my wildest dreams.

My loving father, who worried too much, but always believed in me.

My brother, who inspired me to write.

My brilliant son, Adrian, who is here because these adventures happened.

# Contents

*Maps of the Author's Journey*

CANADA

Stratford

UNITED STATES

MEXICO

HONDURAS

GUATEMALA
EL SALVADOR     NICARAGUA

COSTA RICA

PANAMA

COLOMBIA

ECUADOR

PERU

Lima

BOLIVIA

PARAGUAY

BRAZIL

ARGENTINA

URUGUAY

Atlantic
Ocean

Amazon River

Pacific
Ocean

N
W      E
S

Author's
ROUTE

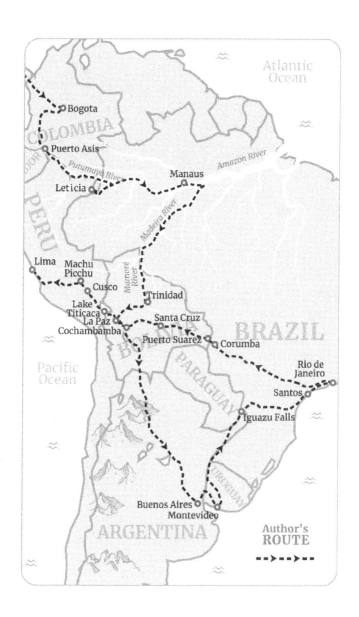

Atlantic Ocean

Bogota

COLOMBIA

Puerto Asis

Putumayo River

Amazon River

Leticia

Manaus

PERU

Madeira River

Lima

Machu Picchu

Cusco

Trinidad

Mamoré River

Lake Titicaca

La Paz

Santa Cruz

BRAZIL

Cochambamba

Puerto Suarez

Corumba

Pacific Ocean

BOLIVIA

PARAGUAY

Rio de Janeiro

Santos

Iguazu Falls

URUGUAY

Buenos Aires

Montevideo

ARGENTINA

Author's ROUTE

# *Prologue*

It is almost impossible to explain how it feels to be lost in the middle of nowhere with no end in sight. Dawn began with the morning songs of exotic wild birds as the sun peeked over our lifeline: the muddy Putumayo River. We ate a meager breakfast of leftovers from supper the night before and set out in our leaky dugout canoe, each taking turns paddling until we became too tired. Exhausted and wondering if we were ever going to find an end to this river adventure, we were rewarded when loud calls from above revealed a brilliantly colored, large flock of red-tailed scarlet macaw parrots flying overhead. Their joyous freedom in flight was contagious. They inspired us to continue on through this everchanging dangerous green wilderness.

This true story of adventure travel tales is a work that was inspired by my overland journey from Canada to Brazil in the 1970s. I set out alone and traveled by every means possible which included buses, hitchhiking, trains, barges, and paddling in dugout canoes.

It is based on my travel journals, original poetry, letters home, remembrances of friends, and my memories as I recall them. I found the time to finally write this book during the COVID-19 pandemic quarantine of 2020.

Adventures shared live forever.

# Chapter 1

# My Journey Begins

### Hitching to Denver

Thanks for the stopping, said the blonde
heading south with the wind
as a beer came from under his seat,
Just one she smiled, drinking
as he talked of horses, cut up bodies, and big rattlesnakes.
Clear lakes passing by, sun bridge falling
both laughing, corn high.
She smiled, put the beer now under her seat
watching Kansas wild sunflowers grow.
For now it was dark and the truck driver called
for a friend or a Holiday Inn,
Denver—she echoed herself in the breeze
So fat trucker stop driving
just find her a ride,
Quick parting, well wishing
old friends of the road.

As a young girl, *The African Queen* was my favorite film. I could imagine myself being Katherine Hepburn, braving the waters of a dangerous river with an earthy romantic hero like

Humphrey Bogart. I longed not for Africa, but South America. I had already made a trip following the overland "hippie trail" from Europe, through the Middle East to India. Now I wanted to explore the Southern Hemisphere of the Americas.

When my friends asked where my next trip would be, I replied, "I am going to explore my Amazonian roots."

My remark was usually met with a quizzical look, questioning my sanity as they asked, "Do you have relatives there?"

People in my hometown of Stratford, Ontario, Canada didn't understand that there was something intangible that attracted me to the yet to be discovered wild places of the Amazon rainforest. This was a personal, private quest that touched my soul, my inner being, my roots. Not genetic roots, *No.* This was a bewitching pull from within the deepest part of me that craved adventure. The Amazon called to me with a powerful voice I could not resist. I had to follow my dream.

\*\*\*

For over a year, I studied the countries and culture of South America as I worked, to save up enough money to make my trip. Fascinated by the exotic wildlife that lived in the tropical rainforests, I fantasized about swimming in the Amazon River with manatees and pink river dolphins. At night I dreamed of entering the heart of the jungle to be the first to discover a long-lost tribe of strong Amazonian women. I imagined myself being invited to join their tribe and become a real Amazon woman. Ready to experience the extraordinary, I longed for real adventure!

On a brisk, sunny September morning at the age of twenty-two, I set out on my solo venture to enter an unknown world and explore the lands that lay between Canada and Brazil. I didn't fly down to Rio, or take an eco-tour. Eco-tours had not even been invented in 1975, nor had Wi-Fi, email, or cell phones. I was completely alone when I left the small Shakespearean festival theatre town where I grew up. From a Greyhound bus I waved goodbye to my concerned parents and was on my way.

***

Crossing the border from Canada to the USA went smoothly. The border guard simply glanced at my passport where I was seated and we were off. As my bus rolled down the road across the United States, my imagination whirled south envisioning the tropical adventures I anticipated. At the end of a 24-hour ride, I left the bus to start hitchhiking, for no particular reason, in Fremont, Nebraska. Yes, it does seem an absurd way to embark on a trip across two continents and yet it was entirely perfect for the gypsy spirit in me. Traveling alone overland gave me the freedom to stop along the way wherever and whenever I chose. The journey truly is as important as the destination.

From Fremont, I hitchhiked south through the United States. The breath of nomadic freedom that can only be achieved when traveling alone filled me with courage. Most of my rides were with friendly truck drivers. The first evening, I found myself in Kansas at sunset being let out of a transport truck in a desolate spot beside a big pile of rocks where the truck driver said he had shot a giant rattlesnake the night before. He explained he had to leave me there because he was afraid his wife or someone he knew might see me in his truck and start rumors if he let me out in the next town where he lived. As he slammed his truck door shut, he shouted, "Watch yerself, girl! A passel of big rattlers lives in them rocks."

I watched him disappear down the highway into the setting sun as a pale, yellow scorpion dashed across the road in front of me. Looking warily over at the ominous rock pile beside me I wondered why he had let me off here. If he wanted to frighten me, he had succeeded. All I could think about as I held out my thumb hoping for another ride was what a good story this will make, and thoughts of writing my tale prevented fear from overtaking my mind. There was very little traffic so I started walking in the hope that if I didn't get a ride, I might at least reach a town or something before it was completely dark. I had no desire to sleep on the side of the road with scorpions and venomous snakes.

Eventually, I did come to a town where I was met with ominous stares from people who could easily have been from the frightening inbred cast of the adventure horror film "Deliverance."

*Was that "Dueling Banjos" I heard being played in the bar?*

This was not the Kansas I remember from the Wizard of Oz. No, I did not relish the idea of spending the night here either, and I was extremely relieved when a truck came along and the driver offered me a ride to the interstate. Here, he assured me, he could find me another ride to Denver. We drank beer in his cab and listened to rock music. After refusing his offer of a night at the Holiday Inn, he used his CB radio to find me a ride to Denver with another truck at the next truck stop. Truck drivers used their CB radios to communicate with each other, to find out about traffic ahead, outsmart the police, or just to chat. He found me offers of rides to San Francisco, Los Angeles, and Texas. I chose Denver, Colorado and arrived downtown at 2:00 a.m. where the YMCA gave me a bed for the night.

\*\*\*

My cousin Katherine, picked me up in Denver the next day and brought me to the hippie college town of Boulder where she was a professor at the University of Colorado. She showed me around the beautiful mountain town, and that evening we shared our poetry.

\*\*\*

From Boulder, I found a ride on the college ride share bulletin board to the Rio Grande River, in New Mexico where I found a lovely place to camp for the night. The Stagecoach Hot Springs were just a two-mile hike along the river, so I set out to find them.

Hiking south on this hot sweltering day over not just rocks, but huge boulders and unexpected deep mud, was exhausting. It took me an hour and a half carrying my heavy thirty-five-pound backpack to finally reach the beautiful, rustic rock-walled hot springs. Immediately I put down my backpack, threw off my clothes and sank naked into the wonderful, warm, bubbling, natural waters. More like-minded people joined me at this idyllic spot. One man played a flute as we sunned ourselves on the surrounding rocks. My new friends offered me a ride to Taos where they lived, so I hiked with them another mile up a steep hill to where their car was parked. As soon as I reached their car, I took off my backpack and before I knew what was happening, I collapsed to the ground like a lifeless corpse. When I came to, one of my new friends was trying to give me water.

"You are dehydrated," he explained. "You need to drink more water."

Lesson learned, I drank as much water as I could and quickly revived.

When we reached their home, they let me pitch my blue tent in their high desert backyard, where the open sky above the Sangre de Cristo Mountains soon filled with thousands of stars to brighten my night. I imagined past explorers lost in the wilderness looking up at the same stars to guide their way. To reassure myself, I whispered, "Thank you, brilliant stars. I trust you to guide my way south. I will succeed in my overland journey to the Amazon!"

\*\*\*

From the enchanting mountains of Taos, I hitchhiked on south to El Paso, Texas on the Mexican border where I spent the night in a cheap, rather sleazy place called Hotel De Soto for $4.50 a night.

The next morning, I picked up my visa from the Mexican consulate and walked across the border into Juarez, Mexico. I had considered taking the $21 bus to Mexico City, but was told by the locals that the train was much better. The train was also a little cheaper at $16, so I decided to take the rail and climbed aboard a gently moving slow train that took three days to reach Mexico City. It was strange being the only person on the train who did not speak Spanish. I felt quite alone until I met two men who also spoke some English. They asked me where I was headed, and I asked them about Mexico. We chatted as best we could in broken English as we rolled down the tracks.

The first day the train passed through mostly dry desert where the only breaks in the landscape were tall cactus. When the train stopped, I bought a basket of ripe, red, delicious, prickly pear fruit through my open window for just two pesos, from a peasant woman making her living by selling food to the train passengers.

The next day we passed through a hilly, more fertile area that was dominated by fields of green corn. At night, armed police came onto the train to search the luggage of all the passengers. They didn't bother with mine though. I suppose it was obvious I was a visitor and not a Mexican.

On the third day, we arrived in Mexico City one minute ahead of schedule. I left the train and walked over to the nearest place to stay, Hotel Nueva Estacion where I rented a room for the equivalent of $4 a night.

This was my first time in Mexico City so I was determined to see some of the sights. From my hotel I took the subway downtown to the National Museum of Anthropology to see the world's largest collection of ancient Mexican art. It was a fantastic museum with an impressive collection that included a huge hand-carved Aztec sun stone calendar, the tomb of the great Mayan ruler K'inich Janaab Pakall, and the ancient jade mask of the Zapotec Bat God believed to have been created as early as 100 BC.

While at the museum, I met three teenage Mexican boys who invited me to visit their home to have lunch. They lived in a modern part of Mexico City in a high-rise apartment building that was protected by armed guards. Their guards reminded me of the police who had come onto my train to Mexico. In the boys' apartment, I found myself surrounded by plastic—plastic on the couches, plastic decorative dolls, plastic tables, plastic clocks, and a stuffed toy dog in a plastic bag in the living room. How disappointing that plastic seemed to have completely replaced the incredible art and culture of their Aztec ancestors.

These sweet, generous boys gave me some lovely Indian beads and because their mother was not at home, the youngest boy made me lunch—canned spaghetti with tacos served, of course, on plastic plates. After lunch, we had fun dancing to Mexican pop songs. I was feeling tired, still they insisted on taking me for a tour of the University of Mexico campus which was very modern with impressive colorful murals on the walls.

My problems started when I went back on the subway to return to my hotel. For at least three hours, I rode every route on the subway trying to find my way back to my hotel. Not only was it extremely crowded because it was rush hour, but I had forgotten to note what subway stop I had started from. I was lost, alone, frightened, and didn't speak Spanish. It was very hot. People were pushing, shoving, and sweating all around me. There was barely enough room to breathe, when I felt a man's hand moving between my legs. *Oh horror!* We were packed in like sardines. *What should I do?*

I managed to squirm away from him and give him an angry glare, when I looked up and recognized the name of my subway stop. Overjoyed, I got off as fast as I possibly could and raced back to the safety of my hotel room, where after killing several bold cockroaches, I fell asleep.

\*\*\*

Enough of the big city! I headed south to a lovely old town called San Cristobal where I was pleased to find the people polite and charming. In my broken English and almost non-existent Spanish, I had a long chat with a friendly young local man on the steps of a beautiful, old church. Our conversation ended abruptly, when a young woman, presumably his wife, arrived and started screaming at me, "Puta! Vete! Puta!"

I attempted to explain to her that we were just talking, but soon realized that she didn't understand a word I said. Granted, I didn't understand what she was saying either, but her message came across loud and clear when she started throwing rocks at me! With tears in my eyes, I ran down the hill back to my hotel room feeling devastated, alone, and completely misunderstood.

Later that day I met Chelsea from Detroit. Like me she was backpacking her way to South America solo. She cheered me up by saying, "Forget that woman. She is a crazy fool," then with a wink added, "Now you can say you were stoned in Mexico."

Her words made me smile. We were both independent young women flitting around the planet like mariposas (butterflies). We even had the exact same birthday April 20, 1953, so we called ourselves "The Mariposa Twin Sisters."

Chelsea suggested we travel south together so we put out our thumbs and spent the next few days hitchhiking all the way from San Cristobal, Mexico to the middle of Guatemala. Our best ride was with an older American man who was driving his pickup truck to Costa Rica where he planned to retire because it would be cheaper living there than in the United States.

When the Spanish arrived in Guatemala in the 1500s, led by Conquistador Pedro Alvarado, they heard the Mayan people call the land Cuautehmallan, but the Spanish could not pronounce it properly so it soon became Guatemala.

Chelsea and I parted ways at Panajachel, Guatemala. She continued south while I remained to explore the hills around Lake Atitlan, a massive body of water in an ancient volcanic crater. We had hoped to meet up later, but sadly it never happened. That is the way of the road. No doubt, my Mariposa Twin Sister is still out there winging her way around the planet somewhere. Traveling alone is the best way to meet new people.

Lake Atitlan was surrounded by steep green hills with quaint Mayan villages. I fell in love with the vibrant indigenous culture that surrounded me. The local people were friendly and dressed in beautiful embroidered native costumes. After bartering with a local woman, I traded my Canadian flag towel, a pair of wool socks, and ten US dollars for two intricately hand embroidered blouses designed with multicolored birds and flowers. We were both pleased with the deal. She was especially excited to get my Canadian flag towel.

The Mayan descendants in Atitlan were remarkable artists, making beautiful designs with thread and material that created a fantasy world of giant corn, live volcanoes, and a primitive lifestyle seemingly protected by no desire to change; however, as the people were finding their art was worth money from tourists, the quality and unique beauty was beginning to be lost by mass production. The "Western" influence that grows first in the cities and then spreads virus-like out in a winding twisting industrial web was slowly making its way here.

\*\*\*

While hiking around Lake Atitlan I met a handsome, blond fellow backpacker named George from Germany, who spoke English fluently and was great fun. We were instantly attracted to each other so we hitchhiked to Guatemala City together where we stayed in Pension Mesa, a popular low budget backpacker's hostel with a lovely central garden and terrible coffee.

George and I spent a lovely week exploring Guatemala's old capitol together. We toured the National Palace of Culture which was both a museum and the headquarters of the president of Guatemala. We enjoyed a fun Canadian Thanksgiving without the traditional turkey, instead, we feasted on rice and beans. We were giddily falling in love. I wanted to visit the spectacular Mayan ruins of Tikal so we made a firm plan to meet again in a few weeks on the island of Flores.

Breathtakingly beautiful, Tikal had been hidden by the ever-growing rainforest for generations and it wasn't until the mid-nineteenth century that European explorers re-discovered it. In 1956, Guatemala created a 575 square kilometer national park to protect not only the thousands of Mayan ruins in the middle, but also a huge expanse of tropical rainforest that was home to a great variety of native fauna. I set up my tent in the campground and spent my days hiking around the impressive ruins of temples and palaces, even climbing to the top of the temple that had been featured dramatically in the first Star Wars film.

I particularly loved watching the wildlife that roamed around the grounds. The animals were not afraid of humans, because hunting was not permitted in the Tikal National Park. Groups of curious ring-tailed coati paraded around my tent trying to peer in, so I kept it zipped up tightly to prevent them and marauding tarantulas from getting inside.

Tikal had been a major Mayan city for over 600 hundred years until it was finally abandoned in the ninth century. Long before the Spanish Conquistadors arrived, the Mayan people had discovered a vast world of knowledge that peaked around the sixth century AD. I studied the hieroglyphics in the ancient stone temples, many of which were still covered with wild, clinging green vines that tried to obscure their message from my sight. Their hidden meaning gripped my heart with a mesmerizing unfathomable power. I wanted to know more, but the creators were long gone. Questions flooded my mind:

*Why was Tikal abandoned?*
*What secrets do the ancient Mayans ruins still hold?*

I could have stayed there for months taking it all in, looking for answers to my questions, but I had promised to meet George and my tent was getting extremely soggy from torrential rains. It was time to pack up and move south toward my ultimate destination: the Amazon.

# Chapter 2

# Jungle Meanderings in Guatemala

*We met in the jungle*

*of twisted minds*

*among dangling Spanish vines,*

*where howlers roar,*

*toucans burrow into rotting trees,*

*and green symbiotic moss*

*kills to reach another source*

As planned, I left the ancient ruins of Tikal to reconnect with George at the inexpensive $2 a night *Hotel Casa Ula* in one of the oldest continuously inhabited settlements in the Americas—"the man-made island of Flores." This lovely island was originally constructed by the Mayans during the thirteenth century. While most of Guatemala was conquered by the Conquistadors in the early 1500s, the Mayans in Flores maintained their freedom until 1697. After occupying it, the Spanish reconstructed the architecture of the island with cobblestone streets and beautiful multicolored buildings of orange, crimson red, and cobalt blue.

George hired a small boat to take us out on the water. He stopped our boat in the middle of the lake just before a beautiful red sunset and proclaimed, "Alycin, I am in love with you. I want you to return to Germany with me. I will build us a concrete dome near the magical Black Forest where we can live happily forever. Will you marry me?"

I had not expected this. I was stunned. I loved him, but I wasn't sure I loved him enough to marry him. I was certainly not ready to get married. Living in a concrete dome in Germany in the winter did not really appeal to me either and to be completely honest, size does matter. I turned him down. Lamentably I told him goodbye and caught the next bus going back to Guatemala City.

***

Lost in my thoughts, on the overcrowded bus, I was surprised when it suddenly came to an abrupt stop after we had only been traveling a short time. I looked out my window to see that we had been brought to a standstill behind a long line of vehicles that were prevented from going further by a huge river rushing across the road ahead. Heavy rains over the past few days had turned what had been a mere shallow stream across the road a week before, into an impassable barrier.

Not prepared to wait to find out how long it was going to take for the turbulent waters to recede, I retrieved my knapsack from the roof of the bus, leaving the rest of the passengers behind, and crossed this newly made rushing river on a narrow rope-and-wood hanging footbridge, with the hope that I might find a ride south on the other side.

After a short wait, I met two burly Guatemalan "Green Police" who were also en route to Guatemala City. They agreed to give me a ride, along with their big truckload of recently harvested mahogany lumber. Guatemala's name comes from the Mayan K'iché language and means "Land of Many Trees" because at one time the country was almost entirely covered by rainforest. Progress always seems to be accompanied by the killing of trees.

Since I had been in Guatemala, I had noticed that there were two kinds of police—the "Blue Police" who were usually friendly and helpful, and the "Green Police," also known as the "Death Squads" who, from what I had heard, carried out whatever dirty work the government found necessary. I was somewhat hesitant to accompany these notorious green-uniformed enforcers of authority all by myself. Still, they seemed nice enough and I wanted to keep going down the road so I trusted my traveler instinct and climbed up into the cab of their 16-wheeler.

Fortunately, my initial concerns were unfounded. Both policemen were extremely polite and kind to me as we bumped and crashed along Guatemala's fifteen-year-old Tikal dirt road. The rough passage proved too much even for this powerful lumber truck. After four hours of jolting past wrecks along the side of the road and a few dangerous near collisions with others, their truck too broke down. Concerned that I might not make the ferry I needed to catch in order to cross the Dulse River before dark, my policeman friends stopped the next passing vehicle, a pickup truck, and ordered the driver to carry me in the back with his cargo the next three miles to the ferry landing. Nobody in Guatemala ever argues with the "Death Squad." The truck driver fearfully agreed. He drove as fast as he could on the rough dirt road so that I arrived just in time to cross the muddy Dulse River, as the glorious Mayan sun set slowly behind us.

***

That evening, while wandering around the little town of Rio Dulse, I met another young woman my age named Carol. I immediately identified her as a Canadian by the small Canadian flag she had sewn onto her backpack. My backpack also had a Canadian flag, not because I was particularly patriotic, but because Canadians were well received pretty much everywhere. Like me she was traveling alone, however unlike me, Carol spoke Spanish. We celebrated our meeting with a cup of *cafe con leche* and shared stories of our travels. Within half an hour we were fast friends.

On an impulse, we decided to buy a canoe and paddle down the Dulse River to Livingston on the Caribbean Sea. Canadians love canoeing and I had never seen the Caribbean before. It didn't matter that we were not quite sure of how long it was going to take or what might lurk ahead in the murky uncharted river waters. We didn't even have a map. It was an adventure, a challenge, and that was enough.

***

The following morning, we searched the town trying to find a cheap, seaworthy canoe. After asking at all the marinas, we were finally taken to a gray-haired, bent over old man who made dugout canoes on the edge of town. He moved slowly as he showed us his canoes. We bargained and after inspecting his entire stock, decided on a small, green dugout for fifteen dollars. After purchasing it, we told him of our plan to canoe to Livingston. Looks can sometimes speak louder than words. Never have I seen such an immediate look of horror on a man's face. The canoe was small and the river was long, but his reaction seemed extreme. He began to tell us stories of the dangers ahead. Carol translated his warning words for me: "You girls can't do this. Three local men went canoeing downstream on this river and were killed for twenty dollars by the natives. The Coast Guard boat will shoot at anything that moves on the water at night—even you!"

Carol began to have second thoughts about our venture. She decided to ask the local police how safe our canoe trip would be and returned with more strange stories. Many people in Guatemala were deeply superstitious and sometimes it was difficult to ascertain how much of what they said was really true. Also, at that time, women in Latin America were not expected to do much more than stay at home and have babies, so Latin macho men didn't believe that women were capable of anything else. I wondered how much of what we had been told was fiction and how much was true. *Were they just trying to frighten us? Did the old canoe salesman feel guilty and responsible after selling a canoe to two crazy gringa women?* The river was calm, our canoe was ready. We decided to go regardless of the discouragement. We both sought an adventure!

***

Our little green dugout looked tiny, after we loaded it down with our backpacks and food, but we still had six inches of freeboard above the water line, and an afternoon of daylight left so we summoned up our courage and set off!

Our weather-worn old canoe maker shook his head slowly as he watched us paddle away. Small settlements of rustic wooden and bamboo houses bordered our way for the first part of our journey. They were soon left behind and replaced by dense rainforest. The farther we traveled, the denser the reaching green tangled shoreline of life became. Gradually the river began to widen into what appeared to be almost a lake. We paddled out into the more open water until a strong wind began to blow, turning what had been glass-like calm water into rough white-capped waves.

I began to fear the environment we had so foolishly thrown ourselves into. My mind returned to a nine-foot-long crocodile I had seen resting on a swampy bank in Tikal not many miles north of where we were. Soon every floating log I saw turned into a smiling hungry croc just waiting to attack our canoe. Our little dugout tossed and rocked dangerously so we headed back toward the shore which was now a tangle of dense green impenetrable vines. We paddled not too close to and not too far from the land. It felt safer canoeing closer to the shore. My courage was beginning to return when suddenly from out of the jungle came the loudest, most terrifying roar I had ever heard in my life.

I turned to Carol and asked, "Was that a jaguar?"

She responded with a silent, blank look of fear.

There was not a sign of civilization anywhere to be seen, a frightening impenetrable jungle with a jaguar to the right and a treacherous widening lake to the left. We had come too far to turn back, so we continued downstream, anticipating the possibility of spending the night in our canoe, clinging onto hanging vines as the shoreline was much too dense here to even attempt a real landing. And we were not about to explore the inaccessible leafy rainforest just to be eaten by a wildcat.

The stormy waters got rougher, so we paddled even closer to the shore into some tall grassy reeds for protection. We continued onward, desperately hoping we might come to a village or at least a place where we could land before the darkness of night overtook us. At the point of giving up, we found what we had prayed for. Just ahead to the right was a little bamboo shelter resting in a small clearing. Quickly we brought our canoe to shore and began to explore. It felt wonderful to have our feet on civilized dry soil again.

Very quickly it became clear that no one had been there for some time. The rainforest had already begun to reclaim this abandoned small plot of land. Nervously, we silently wondered what wild animals might be watching us from the tall vegetation that surrounded us. Still, it was a place on dry land to rest for the night. We were tired and hungry after our long day's journey of canoeing so we retrieved some bread and cheese from the canoe and ate it for supper. After this quick cold meal, we decided to explore our little clearing more to at least find a spot to set up my tent. It looked as though someone had tried to settle here in the rainforest beside the Dulse River once and had eventually given up, leaving the land to be reclaimed by its original natural master. I suspected someone would return again, however, because in the primitive shelter, hidden under a dry palm leaf, I could see a small dugout canoe. I wondered if the dugout in this rustic bamboo shelter was still watertight, so I lifted the palm covering to see the bottom of the canoe.

Carol heard my terrified scream as I jumped backward. In the bottom of the canoe looking angrily up at me was an enormous spider the size of my hand, waving bright yellow claws above a brilliant orange body. That canoe could rest forever as far as I was concerned. At this point, all I wanted to do was put up my tent and get into it for the night. We cautiously poked around with long sticks inside the abandoned bamboo shelter and carefully cleared a place to hurriedly set up camp. Mosquitoes were finding us now, so I thought it was a good idea to start a fire and burn the leftovers from our supper to create some smoke to scare them off. I was too late. Thousands of red ants were already carrying off the remains of our meal.

We crawled into our sleeping bags inside my nylon tent and prepared for a night's rest. I had barely closed my eyes when the same terrifying loud deep guttural growl that we had heard earlier in the day roared from the jungle nearby our tent. The jaguar must have followed us! Another roar now from the other side. There must be more than one, then another roar! It was a jamboree of hungry jaguars! Futilely, I lit a candle, hoping its tiny flame might drive them away. Jaguars have the most powerful bite of all the big cats. Their teeth are strong enough to bite through the thickest hides of crocodiles and the even harder shells of turtles. We were doomed!

Carol began to laugh hysterically. I thought she had gone completely mad with fear; however, it turned out that she had suddenly remembered that she had heard that same very loud roar before in Brazil. It had taken a moment for her to recognize that we were hearing not the roars of hungry jaguars, but the roars of a troop of howler monkeys instead.

We must have inadvertently invaded the territory of these medium-sized monkeys that are famous for their booming, amazingly loud roars. They were up in the trees all around us, trying to scare us away. The monkeys were probably more afraid of us than we were of them. Carol and I both laughed with relief. We were safe. As we lay in our sleeping bags under the skimpy protection of my blue nylon tent, we listened to the unfamiliar night lullaby of jungle sounds that grew louder and louder. Every insect, bird, and animal nearby made its presence known to us by joining the howler monkey chorus in the deepening night.

\*\*\*

I must have finally fallen asleep because the arrival of morning brought renewed strength. Encouraged by the light of day we set off again for Livingston and the Caribbean.

We giggled as we remembered the warning words of our canoe salesman. He may have believed his stories of great danger, but he probably had also never traveled as far east on the river as we were now. I surmised that fear kept him from exploring further. People then, and today, continue to fear the unknown as much now as they did in the time of the early European explorers when the earth was still considered flat. I wondered what discoveries might be made in every realm, if all of us could bring ourselves to go beyond our fears.

As we paddled quietly along the river, we noticed, not too far ahead, a slow puff of smoke coming out of the rainforest.

I asked Carol, "Do you think that is a new settlement up ahead?"

Before she could answer, suddenly, out of nowhere, a huge canoe appeared with six strong men paddling swiftly and directly toward us.

In a slightly hysterical but hushed voice, Carol blurted out what we were both thinking: "Were the old man's stories of murderers true? Is the smoke we just saw where these killers live? Will they rob us or kill us? What should we do?"

Very soon they were going to reach us and there was nothing we could do. There was no place to hide in a canoe on a river and they were moving much faster than we could, so we continued paddling on to bravely meet our fate. Closer, closer, the killers were upon us. I held tightly onto my paddle; the only semblance of a weapon available. They quickly came alongside our small craft and our would-be murderers gave us a friendly smile, waved, and rapidly passed us by. Embarrassed, almost disappointed, we paddled on.

A few hours downstream, a clearing appeared on our right. Three small half-naked children saw us approaching and ran to the edge of the river waving and smiling. The afternoon wind was blowing up again so we decided this might be a safe spot to come ashore to stop for lunch. Our landing place was the home of two very friendly indigenous families that lived by the river in small bamboo huts surrounded by banana and orange trees. They were entertained by us and asked questions in their native language that we did not understand, so we smiled back at them and shook their hands. They seemed to be quite astonished and amused that two white gringa women were canoeing alone in their part of the river. Still, they could not have been more gracious and generously gave us some bananas to eat and stayed with us until we set off.

The afternoon wind continued to blow so we stayed close to shore, paddling through tall brown reeds and past tiny tropical islands. Eventually, the river began to narrow. As it did, the current became stronger so we rested our sore arm muscles and let the river carry us downstream toward the sea. To our left, magnificent white rocky cliffs appeared, stretching up a hundred feet, while long moss-covered vines reached down from the unseen jungle top, sometimes touching our dugout in their attempt to reach water. The lush green, ever-growing forest of life to our right occasionally opened up briefly to show a small settlement. We lay back in the canoe enjoying the sweet sunshine, delighted with our newfound paradise. Now we only had to use our paddles to direct our course while the Dulse River leisurely swirled us around occasionally in one of its slow-moving whirlpools. We floated gently downstream.

Hours passed quietly as we shared the wandering river with colorful water birds. Occasionally a pandemonium of noisy parrots called to us as they flew overhead. Resplendent quetzals, the sacred bird of the Mayans, replied from deep within the rainforest as bright large-beaked toucans watched us curiously from giant trees on the shore. Fortunately, in the late 1980s, Guatemala had made the part of the Dulse River we were exploring into a national park to preserve its unique wildlife and habitat that we were enjoying so completely.

We were beginning to wonder if our magical Dulse River was going to continue on so pleasantly forever when unexpectedly, out of the jungle vines ahead, a great white mass appeared in the distance. *What is it? Could we have finally reached the sea? Yes!* As we grew closer, the Caribbean became a vast beautiful unending expanse of azure blue salt water with cresting waves. Feeling like new-world explorers, we leisurely paddled to the river's mouth, pulled ashore, and stretched out on a beach at our destination of Livingston, Guatemala, in Amatique Bay. We luxuriously relaxed in the warm sand, soaking up the glowing sun as we relived the memories of our marvelous little jungle escapade. I wondered what future adventures awaited me on my journey south toward the Amazon.

# Chapter 3
# *Clemencia in Costa Rica*

### *San Jose*

*Went to the window,*

*there*

*was*

*a*

*boy,*

*his name unknown*

*hiding under a plastic sheet*

I missed the friendship and closeness I had shared with George in Guatemala and wondered if we would ever meet again. But that was not to be. Sometimes things are special because they don't last.

Traveling alone, as I often did, I met new people almost every day. Some I traveled with for a short time and never saw again. Others became lifelong friends. The great thing about being on the road alone is that when you meet new people, they accept you as you are. You can be yourself or whatever self you choose to be. You are no longer seen or judged by your past. I find that incredibly liberating.

A strong wave of homesickness passed over me. I missed my family immensely. I felt stuck—in the middle of the narrowest part of Central America, in its smallest, most densely populated country, El Salvador. Ben, the Algerian man I was now traveling with, had arranged for us to stay with his friends in a slum neighborhood of the capitol, San Salvador. They had no indoor plumbing and shared an outhouse with several other families. Their rustic latrine was located behind their house and only accessible by carefully crossing a narrow, wooden walkway elevated over the pig's muddy enclosure. Ben's kind friends were generous with the very little they had, but it was not a place I wanted to remain for long.

We left San Salvador, hitchhiking south, and got a good ride with a Nicaraguan truck driver. He took us right across hilly Honduras and dropped us off in a small border town in Nicaragua.

***

Our next ride took us south past Lake Nicaragua, the largest lake in Central America and famous for its big freshwater sharks, all the way to the capital, Managua. The driver let us off late at night in a bad part of town, at a cheap hotel that turned out to be an extraordinarily busy whorehouse! I later learned that if you ask for a "cheap" hotel in Spanish they think you mean a brothel. It was horrible, full of giant roaches, stinky toilets, and moaning men being serviced by prostitutes all through the night. The walls of the rooms did not reach the ceiling so we could hear everything in the rooms next to us. Everything! Between clients we could even hear the prostitute next door washing her privates in a basin of water. I tried to take a shower, but was attacked by two inch-long flying roaches when I turned on the water, so I gave up. Exhausted and dirty I got no sleep that night.

Ben was a nice guy, but an absolute bore. He wanted to be my constant companion and take care of me, however he had stopped communicating with me, because I was not interested in being his lover. Spending the night in a whorehouse had encouraged him, but completely turned me off. I longed for the freedom of solo travel again. The Amazon continued to call with a strong, unrelenting voice, so I left on my own the next day and hitched a ride to San Jose, Costa Rica.

\*\*\*

In San Jose I met Clemencia, a beautiful, indigenous woman my age, who approached me on the street to ask me to write a letter for her in English. I was happy to help her and in no time, we became friends. She spoke English fairly well, but was insecure about her writing skills in her second language. That night we stayed at San Jose Hotel Astoria which cost only $1.30 a night with a private hot shower. It was a reasonably decent hotel, especially after the whorehouse in Nicaragua. We had not been in the room long when Clemencia said she needed to go out. She did not make it back to the room we shared until dawn the next morning. I asked her where she had been, but she avoided my question and invited me to visit her papa's farm high up in the San Carlos mountainous rainforest. The idea of traveling deep into the jungle with someone who knew the lay of the land sounded fantastic. I readily agreed.

When the Conquistadors arrived in Costa Rica in the early 1500s, many of the indigenous tribes retreated deep into the heavily treed mountains for safety, to avoid slavery and taxation. They never gave in to the Spanish and refused to be subjugated. In the 1970s it was still possible to disappear into the Costa Rican rainforest; few questions were asked and the indigenous people that became squatters up in the hills were a law among themselves.

\*\*\*

We set off with her handsome brother, Jairo, from San Jose by bus to San Carlos in the mountainous Alajuela Province. Three long bus rides later we were dropped off to walk on a quiet dirt road bordered by banana trees and small farms. As darkness approached, I could see the rainforest just ahead of us. Unlike today, back in 1975 the majority of Costa Rica was still in its natural forested state.

Walking up the muddy mountain road with my heavy backpack was not easy. Clemencia suggested we ask to stay the night at a small house we were passing, because she said as darkness fell, the jaguars came out to prowl and it was too dangerous to keep going. I laughingly agreed, mistakenly presuming that she was just trying to scare me and at the same time wondering if what she said about jaguars might be true.

We spent that night with a friendly family of six. Their little wooden house was very clean with one bedroom, a kitchen, and living room. The floor was brightly polished. One of their older girls stood on two brown, dried coconut shells making twisting movements to shine their wooden floors. They fed us tortillas and beans for supper. We put our bedding down on their living room floor and were rocked to sleep that night by the steady sound of heavy rain falling on their tin roof.

\*\*\*

At sunrise, they gave us strong black coffee and corn tortillas before we set off again on the muddy dirt road toward Clemencia's family's mountain home. It was very hot and my backpack was feeling extra heavy when we came to a huge rushing river in a deep canyon. I could hear the river before we could see it. The only way to cross to the other side was by walking across a flimsy swinging bridge made of knotted rope hanging precariously sixty feet above the roaring water.

Two young men were about to cross toward us from the other side. The bridge could only take one person at a time, so we waited and watched. They tied up their pack horses on the far side of the river and removed their cargo of 100-pound bags of coffee beans which they then carried on their own backs, across the wobbly bridge.

Confused as to why they were doing this, Clemencia explained to me, "The coffee beans need to be kept dry."

The men set down their bags of beans, greeted us in a friendly manner, and crossed back on the rope bridge to get their horses. I wondered how they would manage. There was no way a horse could cross on that bridge. They led their horses down into the ravine, where they proceeded to swim across the river with their horses. I was worried as I watched. Even the horses were having a difficult time crossing this rushing river. They made it across safely though, loaded up their horses again, and continued on their way to town to sell their harvest of green coffee beans.

Before we crossed over, Clemencia told me about the time her father had nearly drowned here, when his horse had slipped in the river below us. With these dangers in mind, we crossed the precarious hanging bridge one at a time, as it swung slowly back and forth, high above the water. This was not an easy task in the humid tropical heat with my heavy thirty-five-pound backpack, but at least I was not carrying a huge burlap sack full of coffee beans! I tried my best not to look down at the rushing river below and made it across safely. Clemencia led us to a natural area of the river that was concealed by foliage and protected by rocks. We were so covered in sweat from the humid heat that we simply threw off our clothes and took a well-deserved swim to cool off.

There were no roads at all anymore, only a muddy jungle trail to follow deeper and deeper into the dense rainforest. We came to a small wooden house on stilts and ate some ripe bananas from a tree in front of it. They were the best bananas I had ever tasted. After a short rest we were off again. My backpack was heavy, and mud clung in clumps to my boots as we climbed higher up into the mountains.

Clemencia's brother, Jairo, said if I married him, he would give me a farm by the river where we could live. He told me that we would never have to worry about anything with wild fruit, bananas, and oranges to eat. Jairo continued, extolling the virtues of growing rice, beans, and corn for tortillas, raising animals for meat, and harvesting wild salads from the jungle. It did sound tempting, however, I knew he was half joking, so I politely refused his offer: "No, gracias."

He laughed and told me I was making a big mistake. Clemencia shook her head and gave me a smile that said *don't pay any attention to my silly brother*.

We continued hiking on, more slowly now, as the trail became steeper and the sweltering heat of the day hotter. We passed a small house by a lake where I heard a very young baby crying. I tried to imagine what it might be like to live and raise a family here.

The vertical trail became more difficult, with sucking mud almost taking off my boots. On both sides and above, we were surrounded by vibrant, green, growing life. I felt swallowed by the enormity of this rainforest. Our narrow muddy path went on and on. It seemed forever, as we trudged up, crossing through streams as we came to them and ducking under small waterfalls that ran across our path down the mountain. I was encouraged to keep moving when a gentle, gloriously cool rain began to fall upon us. I recognized some of the plants that were growing on either side of us as giant tropical versions of the houseplants people grew at home in pots! The steamy, clean, oxygenated air from the plants made me feel like I didn't need to breathe anymore. The plants were doing it for me. I felt more alive than I had ever felt before in my life.

Eventually we reached the top of a mountain where we could look across and see their family's home on the next mountain top.

Unexpectedly, like Tarzan, Jairo let out a loud, wild, jungle cry: "*Ahheeee!*"

I stopped in my tracks and looked at him, surprised and confused.

Moments later another slightly different cry echoed back to us from across the divide: "*Ahhee-aaa!*"

Clemencia saw my confusion and explained, "These are our family calls. They let my family at home know we are coming. When they call back, we know it is safe to proceed."

Like a pack of wolves in the wilderness with a secret language, they called back and forth. I was enchanted.

We climbed down the final muddy jungle slope, crossed another river, and ascended the last mountain to reach the house where their mother greeted us warmly. She was a beautiful, thin woman with long black hair, who, with Clemencia's father, was raising ten children, as well as one adopted child in this jungle paradise. Everyone looked strong and healthy. Completely worn out from the long hike I felt like a sick cow in comparison.

Their small primitive house raised on stilts was made entirely from boards they had cut from nearby trees. The tin for the roof had been carried by hand for two days through the same jungle path we had used to get here. The biggest room was the kitchen. It was at the back of the house and had a slatted floor so when food was dropped, the chickens and pigs that roamed freely under the house could eat what fell. Nothing was wasted. They slaughtered a wild hog in celebration of our arrival and hung it up from a beam in the kitchen to butcher it. The blood draining from the pig's jugular vein fell through the spaces in the wooden floor to the earth below, where their chickens foraging under the house quickly gobbled it up.

Their isolated mountain farm was completely self-sufficient. This indigenous family lived independently very much the way their ancestors had lived for thousands of years. The house was surrounded by the bananas, corn, rice, and beans that they grew. They raised ducks, chickens, turkeys, and pigs for meat as well as a few cows for milking. Bees were kept for honey and the beeswax was used to make candles which was their only light at night. They had no electricity. A nearby waterfall made the most beautiful refreshing outdoor shower. A series of hollow bamboo poles brought a constant stream of running water into the kitchen sink. The rest of the world could disappear, and it made no difference up here in their remote tropical kingdom.

One of Clemencia's older sisters who lived nearby came to visit with her eight-year-old twin boys. These children had lived their entire life in the rainforest. They had never even seen a car. Pack horses were the only transportation they knew.

Their home was surrounded by a dense, pristine, virgin tropical forest filled with abundant wildlife. I began to learn first-hand about the native edible and healing plants that grew nearby from Clemencia's mother. She knew what every plant could be used for. Slowly, I was learning how to live a truly self-sufficient life in the rainforest.

I asked her if their ancestors had made any pyramids like the Aztecs in Mexico, or the Mayans in Guatemala. She smiled knowingly and told me about some mysterious huge, perfectly round stones found further south in Costa Rica near the Terraba River. She explained that in ancient times the elders used to assemble around these giant stone spheres to receive advice from their Gods. Later, I learned that there are at least 300 of these remarkable huge stones. Some weigh as much as fifteen tons and no one today knows how they were made, or even moved. They remain one of Costa Rica's secrets of the ancients.

Clemencia's parents were incredibly warm and kind to me. They even invited me to stay for Christmas. After a few wonderful weeks though, I was forced to head back to San Jose to renew my Costa Rican visa, so Clemencia and I made the trek back together. One of her cousins joined us for part of the hike with her newborn son. This was when I saw my first wild black jaguar. It tracked us for several hours, as we made our way along the winding jungle path. Scarlet macaws overhead warned us when it got too close. Occasionally, we saw a glimpse of the big cat stalking us, then magically, it disappeared into the greenery again. Clemencia said it was following us because we had a new baby with us and it could smell her cousin's still-flowing birthing blood. Once, the big cat's round yellow piercing eyes met with mine. I stood still and couldn't move, but Clemencia said to be safe we had to keep moving steadily forward, so we did.

Jaguars are the largest cat native to the Americas and the third largest in the world after tigers and lions. Sadly, today, primarily due to habitat loss and poaching, the jaguar's mere existence is threatened. Being stalked by a wild jaguar was one of the most exhilarating experiences of my life. I wouldn't trade it for anything.

Eventually, we arrived at another cousin's house closer to the river. This family was very poor and the only food they had in their house were two eggs. Costa Rican people are incredibly generous. Everywhere we went they insisted on feeding us. Her cousin cooked her last two eggs for us. I quietly told Clemencia I was not hungry. She told me that to refuse the food they offered us would be an outrageous insult, so we began to eat very slowly. Her cousin's two young children stared silently at us as we ate. They were obviously very hungry. I felt incredibly guilty. Not only was I eating their only food, I wasn't even hungry. When her cousin stepped out of the house for a moment, Clemencia passed her plate to one of the children. I did the same. The children immediately and ravenously ate what was left on our plates. When their mother came back into the house, we gave the empty plates back to her and she was none the wiser. Her children shared a secret smile with us.

As we continued back along the jungle trail, every house continued to feed us. I couldn't eat another bite, but I forced myself to eat to be polite. Clemencia even threw up on the side of the trail she was so full! We hiked on together and crossed the narrow rope bridge that took us back to civilization.

\*\*\*

In due course, we made our way back to San Jose where I renewed my visa. I really liked Clemencia and her wonderful family, who had been extremely kind and generous to me. I had planned to return, but sadly never did make it back to her family home deep in the mountainous rainforest. I feel forever fortunate to have lived, for a short time, in the mountains with the ancestors of these mysterious, independent people.

Clemencia was a fascinating, perplexing young woman who didn't seem to truly fit into either her family's primitive lifestyle in the mountains, or the big city of San Jose which is where I saw her last. She never actually said it, but in retrospect, I suspect she made her money in San Jose as a prostitute.

# Chapter 4
# Orchids of Our Jungle in Pueblito

*Children open slowly,*

*so very slowly,*

*Orchids of our jungle*

Outside, the sky was opening up with the first rays of daylight peeking through. Roosters awakened, calling with their first crow for the sun to rise in the sky. A single horse could be heard in the distance trotting at a mad pace down the black hard road to the village of Paraiso. I was in Costa Rica, the last country before I reached the Panama Canal, living at Pueblito, a village for abandoned children, which became my home for a time before I continued on to South America.

I reflected on my travels south from Guatemala to El Salvador, through the rolling green mountains of Honduras, next to Nicaragua, with its strange earth-shaken capital of Managua. I had traveled on my own by bus or by car, whatever ride came my way until I reached Costa Rica. The attentions of "Macho" Latin men were often unbearable and the only way to tolerate them and survive was to ignore them. Still, at times, the pressure was too much and I found myself striking out verbally in anger.

For the most part though, the warmth, kindness, and generosity of the Costa Rican people was overwhelming. I had learned that people here would share their last morsel of food and go hungry themselves to do it. They were simple, earthy people who worked hard, living, it appeared to my twenty-two-year-old self, a life without the luxuries of emotional hang-ups or unnecessary worry. In many ways though, I also found their life narrow and mundane. It made me miss the spiritual perspective of life I had found during my travels in India a few years earlier.

Local folk art didn't seem to really exist in Costa Rica, especially compared to Guatemala, with the exception of the diminishing colorfully painted ox carts that could occasionally be seen rolling down country roads. These brightly painted ox drawn wagons had originated with Italian immigrants from Sicily and were initially used in the 1800s to haul coffee beans over the mountains to the ocean ports for export. I found it very sad that in this area where the original Mesoamerican people had grown and flourished, so little of their presence appeared to be left.

I wondered what Costa Rica was like when the indigenous people were the ones in charge. I wanted to explore the history of their culture and try to find the parts of it that could be saved, before being entirely lost. There didn't seem to be many of the original indigenous people left in Costa Rica. Perhaps that is why it was the first Central American country to attract the material American world, leaving behind the past without really looking back. Now only about 2% of the country's population is indigenous. They didn't gain the right to vote until 1994, and still suffer from discrimination.

It appeared to me that only the art of the wealthy class was recognized. At first glance, there seemed to be nothing else. But occasionally, I met a rare true artist in some remote village like a man I met in Paraiso who painted for no other reason than because art was a beautiful part of himself that needed to be expressed. He invited me into his home to see his paintings. They were colorful and unique, showing an almost childlike perception. It reminded me of a boy I knew in India. His mother had come to Swami Gitananda at Ananda Ashram where I was studying yoga. She complained about her lazy son and asked for Swami Gitanada's advice. She said her son refused to work in the fields. All he wanted to do was paint! Swami Gitananda, recognizing his artistic talent, invited the young man to live at the ashram where he spent his days painting murals of Hindu Gods on the walls of the ashram.

My travels so far had been fascinating, but it was not enough. I wanted to help, not just visit. I wanted to try to make a difference in the lives of the poor children I saw on the streets of San Jose. Prior to leaving Canada, I had heard a CBC radio show where Canadian Peter Tacon, spoke passionately about helping Costa Rica's orphans with a joint Canadian/Costa Rican project called Pueblito Canada, A Village for the Children. Near Paraiso, Costa Rica, Peter was building Pueblito, a new home for deserted and mistreated children aged three to fourteen from the streets of San Jose and Cartago. It was being set up as a cooperative of group homes with nine houses.

\*\*\*

From San Jose I took a two-hour bus ride to Pariaso, and offered to help. Pueblito was still under construction. A few of the already built homes housed two parents with eight to ten abandoned children to raise as their own. The children lived in these family groups with a couple who had agreed to be their parents. When a child came into one of these families they got not only parents, but uncles, aunts, and cousins, all the relatives of that particular couple—a real family. Family is everything in Costa Rica.

If you have ever left North America and traveled to any Third World country, you will have seen lost children in small groups or alone on the street. Some are selling cheap articles and others are begging or crouching fearfully in doorways. They are the unwanted children of the poor, the mistreated victims of human torture; children who have been abandoned in the city by families too poverty stricken to feed them and left to make it on their own by stealing, scavenging in garbage, and engaging in prostitution. They are the rejects on the outskirts of a society incapable of caring for them. The children at Pueblo were amazingly strong, independent little souls. They had been on the streets alone and managed one way or another to survive.

The children all had different, but very sad stories. Some had been found on sidewalks, others in jails. Many of the children did not know their last names or birthdays. Little Maria had been kept like an animal in a cage in her family's backyard because she was "a bother." She had been starved and fed only scraps. When she arrived she was extremely thin. Maria ate as much as she could and in a short time became a chubby little girl. Her growth in height had been permanently stunted by her previous starvation so she was short for her age. Another girl had machete marks on her arms inflicted by her father who had also violated her. Jose, eight, had been keeping his younger brother and sister alive on the streets all by himself for a year by begging and stealing. Sylvia, seven, and her five-year-old brother had been living out of garbage cans. I grew very close to one six-year-old boy named Luis. If I had been older, I would have adopted him, but in Costa Rica you must be twenty-five years old to be considered as an adoptive parent. I was just twenty-two. He had been abandoned to the streets by his prostitute mother because her new man didn't want him around.

These children were not "children" as we think of them. Physically and emotionally they were young, but their experiences went beyond most adults. Even with their horrid backgrounds, the children at Pueblito were affectionate, loving, and eager to learn or help whenever they could. In many ways the children seemed quite mature but, as I got to know them better, I learned that they were emotionally very immature. During their life on the streets they had needed to be completely focused on their instinct to survive, while their true feelings and emotions had to be suppressed to enable them to prevail. In Pueblito they had advantages they had never known before, enough to eat, a home with loving foster parents and new brothers and sisters. This new way of life slowly allowed them to become children again.

# Orchids of our Jungle in Pueblito

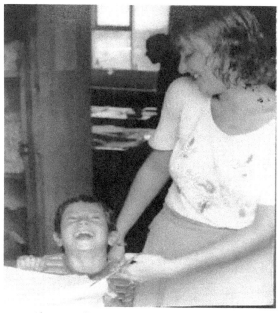

*Alycin and Luis having fun doing arts and crafts
at Pueblito in Costa Rica.*

I volunteered to be the Coordinator of Recreation, which meant I was to do art projects with the kids. I started with drawing and painting classes with the children. Their paintings were incredibly powerful. Most of them had never painted or been exposed to any art form before. On sunny days, I took the children out into the fields where we danced freely to recorded Peruvian flute music. At first they were shy, but soon they started to feel the music with me and we all danced together in the grass with total abandon. The phrase "dance like nobody's watching" would have applied well here. The children became completely carefree as they moved, enjoying new music and freedom to be their true selves.

AMAZON HITCHHIKER

\*\*\*

One night, I took seven of the children to the National Theatre of Costa Rica in San Jose. It is an old theatre designed after the Paris Opera House with ornate golden chandeliers and magnificent murals on the walls. I contacted the theatre in advance and they generously donated a balcony box seat for the children of Pueblito to see a production of Sleeping Beauty. As we sat together in the grand old house, it felt like an Oliver Twist story come true for the children. Most of them had never even seen television before. They were completely mesmerized with their little eyes as big as saucers while they watched the costumed actors on the stage. They loved live theatre and the play. It took them to a fantasy world they had never before imagined.

During their short, impoverished lives on the streets, these children had never seen, or even imagined anything like the pageantry and beauty of this play. Having grown up backstage while my parents worked at the Stratford Shakespearean Festival, I knew that theatre for them would be real magic. I believe that exposing these children to the arts, who had known nothing but neglect and abuse, opened their minds and imagination to new possibilities for themselves that they had never thought of or considered before.

\*\*\*

The children at Pueblito had no toys. So, as Christmas was approaching, I asked what gifts the children would receive from St. Nicholas. Sadly, there was nothing in the budget for toys. I had worked to save money for this trip by making wooden toys the previous winter in Canada, so I decided to make toys for all

42

of the Pueblito children. I started by scavenging for leftover wood at the construction site where the new houses for Pueblito were still being built. I took the two-hour bus ride to San Jose to find the wood glue I needed. To avoid using nails that might scratch or poke the children I also needed wooden dowels. There weren't any to be found. With the help of a Spanish interpreter, I had a talk with a carpenter in the nearby village of Paraiso. He agreed to make some wooden dowels for my toys. All the materials now gathered together, I needed a real workshop where I could make them. After a few inquiries I found out that the local Paraiso High School, that had loaned the land on which Pueblito was being built, had a wood workshop.

I got permission to use the workshop tools and the next day I began to make toys. Being an attractive, young, blonde Canadian woman, I made quite a hit in this Latin American high school wood shop. I was probably the first female to ever use it. Six months had passed since I had last used a bandsaw so I was a little bit nervous as I made my first cut with a crowd of amazed teenage boys all around me. I sawed with careful accuracy though and soon I had the respect and encouragement of all. They opened their shop for me to use the power saws, sanders, and drills whenever I wanted.

Not to be outdone, when the carpenters working on the new Pueblito buildings heard that I was making wooden toys for the kids, they decided they would try too. They were heard saying, "If a crazy gringa can do it ... so can we!"

After an eleven-hour workday, these kind men spent an extra hour or two every evening creating their own toys for the children. That year when St. Nicholas flew, every child at Pueblito received a beautiful handmade wooden toy. If I close my eyes, I can still imagine the youngsters' laughter as they joyfully played in the early light of Christmas Day with their first ever new toys.

Given the opportunity, I believe that most people are generous and kind, because the rewards of giving to one who truly appreciates their gift, is one of the most delightful experiences life can give. I will never forget those amazingly resilient children who will have now grown up to have families of their own.

# Chapter 5

# *Bogotá, Colombia*

*Goodbye Safeway*

*With your toilet paper smiles*

*Farewell to lovers with cynical words*

*I open wider, deeper than the grandest canyon*

*Floating on a river undisturbed*

*by loud mumblings of egos*

*dangerous voices*

*What was left behind is found again*

*Tottering on the other side*

It was getting close to Christmas, a very special time in my family and I was feeling a new wave of homesickness. Long distance phone calls were prohibitively expensive. I had asked my parents to send letters to me at the Canadian Embassy in the city that I anticipated arriving next, because the embassy would hold your mail until you could pick it up or forward it to another embassy if you could not. When I was in Mexico and Guatemala, I asked my family to send my mail to the Canadian Embassy in Bogotá, Colombia. Consequently, I often went months without any communication from my friends and family. Phones where one could make long distance calls were very expensive and hard to find. This lack of contact left me longing for home, but it also helped me to begin to grow into a stronger, more independent woman.

Originally, I had planned to travel overland all the way to South America, but when I got to Panama, I learned that there was no road through the Darien Gap to Colombia. So, after traveling south through the Americas for nearly five months, I arrived in Bogotá on a late-night plane from Panama. I was incredibly excited to finally be in South America.

While waiting to go through Colombian customs, I met a friendly Columbian family there to pick up their son who had been studying at the University of Texas in Austin. They invited me to come to stay at their home in a Bogotá suburb, for a reasonable weekly fee of $15 that included room and board with a private bedroom. I had no other advance arrangements, so I readily agreed, thinking this would help improve my Spanish and be a fantastic introduction to Colombian life too.

Soon we were in their car driving through a chilly rain to their home. I had expected it to be tropically warm in Colombia, but here in the high altitude of Bogotá it was disappointingly cold. They immediately offered me the run of the house, food, a hot shower, and a clean bed, all of which I gratefully accepted. Their home was a modern two-story building with four bedrooms upstairs and a kitchen, living, and dining room on the ground floor.

Colombia seemed very hospitable so far. I was glad to be traveling unaccompanied. Surprisingly, I found that being a single woman traveling alone was actually safer than traveling in a group, because everyone I met wanted to take me in and help me. Accepting the kindness of strangers is a wonderful part of the magic in being a solo wanderer.

My new middle-class Colombian family immediately adopted me as one of their own. I started to contemplate living with them long enough to take a Spanish course at the Bogotá University.

Senora Gonzalez, the mother of the household, worked constantly, doing everything she possibly could for her children and husband. Continuously working with her was their little live-in maid Maria who slept in a room behind the kitchen and never got a day off. She was thirteen, but looked more like an eight-year-old child and apparently got this job because she was a poor relation from rural Colombia. Hunched over, talking to herself in a private fantasy world, Maria washed the family clothes by hand every day, in icy cold water that chapped her petite little hands to the point of bleeding.

The father of my new family, Dr. Gonzalez, was a typical macho master of the household. He did as he pleased. The rest of the family all obeyed his orders without question. To amuse himself in front of me he teased their little Pekingese dog by repeatedly dropping small things on it. I was horrified. Even though he was a doctor, I was the one who had to draw his attention to their poor servant girl's sore hands and insist that she be given some kind of medication to treat them. He seemed completely oblivious and unsympathetic to her situation, but under my persuasion did get her some antibiotic cream for her hands.

I took a city bus downtown to get my mail and visit the fantastic Bogotá Gold Museum. It contained more than 55,000 pieces of gold artifacts from all of Colombia's major pre-Hispanic cultures. At one point a door was opened and we were led into a completely dark room. When the lights were turned on, we found ourselves surrounded by a 360-degree display of solid gold relics. It was breathtaking. As the visitors left the room, I stayed on, studying the beautiful gold sculptures. Before I realized what was happening, the door had been shut again and the lights were turned off. I stood alone, silently feeling the powerful energy of the ancient peoples who had created these gold works of art. When the guide returned, he was quite shocked to see me alone in the gold room. At first, I think he thought I might have been a thief, but soon realized nothing was missing and made sure I left when he closed the door again.

The women in the household where I was staying were not allowed out of the house after dark without a chaperone, and that included me. In a short time, I became as paranoid about going out alone as everyone else in the family. I ended up staying in Bogotá for both Christmas and New Years of 1976, even though I was really beginning to hate the city's rainy, cold weather.

On a rainy midnight Christmas Eve, the entire family gathered together, not around a Christmas tree, but around a nativity scene made of plastic and ceramic figures. After the family had gathered, the father read a passage from the Bible, as in turn did each male member of the family. Following the reading everyone opened the gifts addressed to them. Due to my poor Spanish, I confused the words "to" and "from" and mistakenly addressed all of the gifts I had for them to myself. It was quickly sorted out to the amusement of all, and my gifts went to whom they were intended. I felt extremely sorry for their little maid, Maria, so I gave her a Spanish copy of "The Christmas Carol" in hopes that by reading this book it might make her life more bearable. I wished I could have done more for her.

I received a few small Christmas gifts: a broach, a box of chocolates, and a tiny stuffed dog which I genuinely appreciated as I had only known this family for a week. After the gifts had been opened, we all enjoyed a huge meal which included soup, meat, and potatoes, followed by a sweet pudding. From then until sunrise everyone danced to lively Colombian music. Dr. Gonzalez was a great dancer. The early American disco song *Rock the Boat, Rock the Boat Baby* by The Hughes Corporation was very popular in Colombia at that time and their teenage daughter, Sofia, played it over and over again between popular Columbian songs. I went to bed around 4:00 a.m. The rest of the family stayed up and danced on until the sun rose. That Christmas morning we ate a breakfast of cheese donuts and pudding. The rest of the day, most of the family slept, while Maria and Senora Gonzales worked constantly to prepare another huge meal for us.

***

It seemed as if I had barely recovered from their wonderful Christmas festivities before it was the end of the year and that was a real party. At midnight on New Year's Eve, 1976, the Colombian National Anthem was played on the radio, followed by the entire family running upstairs to change into yellow underwear for good luck in the New Year. As I didn't own any yellow underwear to change into, I wondered if I would still have good luck in the New Year.

The party proceeded with fireworks and everyone danced and drank and danced more in their living room. At 4:00 a.m., I was surprised when a delicious meal of Chinese food was delivered to our table. We ate and the dancing continued, as did the drinking until the sun came up.

\*\*\*

On New Year's Day, I was suffering from a terrible hangover mixed with homesickness. I spent most of the day in bed feeling as if this might be my last day on earth, swearing I was never going to drink again. Amazingly, the rest of the family continued partying throughout the day! I couldn't believe it. After all that partying and food, I decided I should reflect and fast on New Year's Day. The birth of the New Year gave me the courage to leave this friendly family and continue on my adventures south. I never saw the Gonzalez family again, but I will forever remember their kindness, Colombian joy in celebration, and love of dance.

\*\*\*

My next stop was the city of Cali, which at that time was a place of culture and the arts, not yet the center of the Colombian drug cartels. Arriving after dark by bus, I was fortunate enough to meet another friendly Colombian family at the bus station. They kindly took me home for the night. Cali was caliente—hot. I loved it. I connected with more new friends in the local theatre and we spent hours talking late into the night about politics and the arts in an outdoor cafe. I even went to see a few plays while I was there, although I didn't understand much of the dialogue due to my limited Spanish.

\*\*\*

From Cali I took a four-hour bus ride further south to Popayan where I stayed in a hostel and met two fellow Canadian backpackers, Suzanne and Janice, who were traveling with an American man, Dennis. Janice and Suzanne were both from British Columbia. Suzanne was twenty, with long auburn hair and Janice was nineteen, with long snow-white blonde hair. With my blonde hair, the three of us attracted quite a bit of attention in Latin America where the norm is black hair.

We decided to travel south together for a while, heading first to the nearby Coconuco thermal hot springs, also known as "Agua Tibia and Agua Hirviendo" (warm water and hot water). In Latin America at that time, hotels and most houses only had showers, never a bathtub, so the idea of soaking our travel worn bodies in the warm springs was very appealing. There actually were two springs, and the hot water spring was so hot it was said you could boil eggs in it. People were literally boiling eggs in the water to prove it! The warm water spring was divine.

After a long, delightful soak in the warm waters, we went for a hike to the top of a hill above the springs. On our way up we met two small rather raggedy-looking children. They lived with their parents in a one-room house that we were passing. Dennis and Suzanne walked over to their house with the children, and Janice and I continued up to the summit of the hill. When we returned, Dennis was turning green and Suzanne was giggling. They explained that they had been invited into the house to eat what was cooking on their fire. They didn't realize until they started eating that they were being fed mice. As soon as we were out of earshot of the family, we all roared with laughter. Dennis was nauseous. Even though I was laughing, I still could not get over the amazing generosity of this poor Colombian family who had nothing but mice to feed their children and were still willing to share this meager meal with strangers.

*** 

The next day we took a bus to nearby Silvia where we boarded another bus bound for Ecuador. My mind wandered as I looked out the dark window of our night bus headed south. I pondered to myself why I was going to Ecuador. I didn't want to just follow the Lonely Planet backpackers "Gringo Trail" to Peru and then Bolivia. I feared I was falling right into line. I wanted to do something more original, more exciting. Little did I know that the next morning I was bound for something completely unplanned.

Janice passed me some valium she had in her bag and took two herself so that we might try to get some sleep on our all-night bus ride south. We still couldn't sleep so instead we sang old Beatles tunes as we rolled down the road giggling, laughing, and sharing our travel stories.

A few seats to the right of us were two handsome young men speaking a language we could not understand. French? No. It wasn't Spanish either. I questioned them as to their origin in my very best, still pitiful Spanish as it was the local language. They answered me in broken Spanish. The tallest one with thick, curly brown hair was named Paulo. His friend Sergio had longer, fairer hair under a very cool Panama hat. We learned that they were Brazilians heading back to Brazil via the Amazon River, with the plan of reaching Rio de Janeiro in time to celebrate Carnaval. They had been speaking Portuguese.

Being a small-town Canadian girl, I had never even heard of Brazilian Carnival before, however the Amazon River sounded fantastic! Janice and Suzanne thought this was a great idea too, because they were supposed to meet Janice's sister and mother in Rio for the annual Brazilian festival of Carnaval at the end of February. Sergio and Paulo's plan was perfect for all of us. Yes, this could be the Amazon adventure I had fantasized about. In what felt to me like a dream coming true, we decided to change buses at midnight in Pasto with the Brazilians, for another bus that was going to take us to some place called Puerto Asis, Colombia, which, according to Sergio and Paulo, was located at the headwaters of the Putumayo River, a tributary of the Amazon. They told us that in Puerto Asis, we could easily find a barge that would take us downstream to the Amazon River and then on to Brazil. The Brazilians were quite surprised at our joining them so suddenly, however, they also seemed rather pleased.

# Chapter 6

# Heading to the Amazon Headwaters

### Who Am I?

Often misunderstood,
I live in a magical, yet solitary faraway place,
Where Chekov's Nina cries from my broken heart.
Tennessee Williams' Laura, sees through my delicate eyes
Shakespeare's Portia speaks with my strong voice.
Shelly is sane—not mad
Van Gogh cut off his ear with good reason,
Beethoven plays brilliantly in silence
Mozart is always a child
Peter Pan visits me at night
Isadora dances eternally with her flowing scarf
Tornadoes spin to take me to the Emerald City
While the place I call home is Camelot
If you bravely dare to ride my Pegasus
I know not what Zeus will do or say
No matter for one day I'll fly away.

We changed buses in the middle of the night for a bus to Puerto Asis. This bus was an overcrowded, old, rickety wreck with not enough seats for all the passengers. For an arduously long ten hours we traveled down a descending, winding ravine dirt road into a world I had never seen before. Sergio and Paulo, being gentlemen or perhaps just trying to impress the Canadian girls, gave us a real seat, while they sat on an extremely uncomfortable piece of wood that had been used to replace a broken seat. I am sure they regretted their kindness after a few hours. The early part of the trip was quite cold, but as we traveled further and further down toward the Putumayo River, the temperature gradually began to increase.

In the dim light of early dawn, I noticed small ferns growing on the roadside among humid green hanging mosses which covered the tall reaching trees that rose on the edge of the road. The opposite side of our roadway stretched down, down, down, seemingly infinitely into a faraway canyon. Our dirt road was frequently crossed by cascading rivers, which with each turn increased in strength and size. There were no bridges on this treacherous route. Not in the least fazed, our bus driver forded each new rushing river that ran across the road. Meanwhile, I watched the roadside ferns grow from six-inch plants to six-foot looming giant tree ferns. It felt like we were traveling on a journey to the center of the earth.

As the sun rose high in the sky, we finally reached Puerto Asis, a frontier town on the headwaters of a tributary of the Amazon River. Barely able to walk we were so tired, we staggered out of the bus and set off with our knapsacks to find a cheap hotel to rest. At the first hotel we inquired in, we were met by a friendly Frenchman, Christian, who began to laugh hysterically when we mentioned that we hoped to catch a boat downstream to Leticia the next day. His uncalled-for laughter made us all think he must be suffering from some kind of jungle madness. Eventually, he regained his composure and sent us further down the street to another hotel because the one he was staying in was full. With a smirk on his face, he said, "See you later." This came as no surprise to me because there was only one street in this little town. We soon found accommodation at the Hotel Monte Carlo for a very reasonable fifty cents a night.

\*\*\*

The following morning, well rested, I awoke ready for adventure. Up and out of the hotel before anyone else, I set off for the docks to find a boat. At the tiny harbor I found our Frenchman, Christian. He was involved in a loud argument with another man, while three very white, odd-looking European types stood nearby listening. Upon seeing me, Christian flamboyantly invited me to join him and explained the situation. I had to laugh. I was thrilled by what he told me. There were no barges traveling downstream on the river now because, being the dry season, the Putumayo River was too shallow to accommodate big boats. Instead, Christian, Jose the Spaniard he was arguing with, and the three Europeans: Bernhardt, a short, stout Austrian, Robert, a handsome, small-framed German, and Ditmar, an extremely tall, lanky man from Switzerland, were all going to buy a canoe and paddle downriver to Leticia.

Bernhardt, Robert, and Ditmar spoke German and very little English. They had all worked together as chefs on a cruise ship. This was their first venture onto dry land off their luxury ship in years. I later learned that not one of them had ever even been in a canoe before.

Christian asked, "Would you and your friends like to join us?"

Immediately, without thinking it through or even considering how far Leticia might be, I agreed and ran off to tell the others. Janice and Suzanne were less enthusiastic than I was, but agreed to join the multinational crew. The Brazilians agreed with me and also thought it was a great idea. From Dennis I received a strange reaction. He behaved as if I had only said "Good Morning" and went on to tell me how cheap avocados were in Puerto Asis. Together we all headed down to the dock to find out more.

That evening just before sunset, all of us, bar Dennis, put our money together and purchased a used twenty-five-foot-long handmade dugout canoe for $85. Our beautiful hand-carved, dugout canoe was so large that the previous owner earlier that day had used it to transport a very young horse to Puerto Asis! It must have been made from an absolutely enormous tree. Dennis was, perhaps wisely, afraid to join our canoe trip. Christian loudly accused him of being the weakest American he had ever met. Dennis looked away and said not a word.

We headed back to our hotel, got stoned on some great Colombian grass and stayed up half the night talking about the adventures we were about to have canoeing in the Amazon Basin. I found an absolutely gigantic hairy spider having babies in the corner of my hotel room and wondered what other strange exotic creatures might be waiting for us in the jungle. Dennis disappeared the next morning before any of us were up. We didn't know what had happened to him until months later,

Suzanne received a postcard from him from Machu Picchu, Peru.

*Jose, Robert, and Bernhardt (in the hats) at Puerto Asis harbor purchasing our dugout canoe to paddle down the Putumayo River.*

The weather was exceptionally hot, wet, and muggy. The Puerto Asis harbor was quite busy with dugout canoes navigating around moored barges as they unloaded cargoes of mostly bananas, which were then packed into carts pulled by horses. Anything that was dropped was immediately eaten by the pigs that roamed along the muddy shoreline.

Janice, Suzanne, and I decided to purchase matching, inexpensive tan "jungle" shirts, straw hats, and rubber boots for our trip. We looked like we were creating costumes for a jungle film, not a real canoe trip into the Amazon Basin. We each sent a postcard home to our parents telling them not to worry if they didn't hear from us for a while, because we were going to go down the Amazon in a dugout canoe we had purchased with seven men we had just met, and might not have access to a post office for a while. Our poor parents! They must have been horrified.

\*\*\*

At sunrise the following day, we gathered by our canoe with our backpacks for the trip. We waited impatiently for the guide that we had hired the day before. When it reached 11:00 a.m., Bernhardt, Robert, and Ditmar were ready to embark on the journey without a guide. It was now obvious that the guide we had hired the day before was not going to show up. The condition of sale when we purchased our dugout canoe was that a guide was included. Apparently, now that we were the owners of the old canoe, the guide no longer felt responsible. He had our money and was gone.

We sat on the dock perplexed as to what to do. We asked a few passing locals if they would like to guide our canoe, but were met instead with stern warnings about huge alligators called caiman, strange currents, giant snakes, poisonous spiders, and cannibal Indians living downstream. We assumed their stories were true because we were in fact headed into what was then, a very remote area of the Colombian jungle. Silently, we wondered. Eccentric Christian wondered too much, and not trusting his own judgment, consulted with the ancient Chinese Book of Changes, the *I Ching*, before deciding against going. Christian's unexpected abandoning of our trip infuriated Jose.

With Christian's sudden departure, Jose, the confident Spaniard, immediately became our self-appointed captain. In no time, this arrogant man soon earned the name of Captain Jose Pizarro after the Spanish conquistador. He waved a machete in the air and promised to kill a tiger on the trip and give me a tooth. I doubted his finding a tiger in the Amazon rainforest, but let him keep his fantasy. Jose then set off promptly to find another guide. I decided at that point I was not going without a guide. The sun was getting very strong, so Robert suggested we build a sort of sun shelter in the middle of our dugout canoe by using wooden poles that we could hang a tarp over if needed on our journey, to create shade or protect us from rain. It was a good idea and gave us something to do until Jose returned.

After a long search another guide was found, an indigenous man who lived downstream en route along the river. For ninety Columbian pesos (which worked out to about $3 a day) he agreed to guide our dugout canoe down the Putumayo River. We loaded backpacks into a mountain in the middle of our still unnamed canoe. Stocky Bernhardt had the largest backpack I had ever seen in my life. It must have weighed seventy pounds. The locals at the dock all agreed that our canoe was going to sink with so much weight. Young, foolish, and brave, we paid no attention to their warnings. Ready for anything, afraid of nothing, I stared ahead trying to see into my unknown future. I thought of my family, and my old friends, and wondered if I was ever going to see them again.

In a very few minutes we left the town of Puerto Asis behind us. On every side all we could see was a growing tangle of solid rainforest. Each person in the canoe took a turn paddling, while our silent guide sat at the back and steered our boat along the winding Putumayo River.

The river current was slow on our first day, so it was fairly uneventful.

At sunset we stopped on the shores of the first farm we found. It belonged to an old couple. They were very happy to see us. The lady of the house, Maria exclaimed, "Usted son aventureras!"

I was charmed. Yes, she had called us adventurers.

My dream was coming true. She invited all ten of us into their home to join them for supper. They ran a generator for electricity and were watching Bonanza in Spanish on their television. When Bonanza was over, they turned off the generator. Their cattle and horses then gathered closer to the house while the jungle sounds outside increased in intensity and volume. The lightning bugs were so abundant, they lit up the surrounding trees like Christmas lights. I think we reminded Maria of her three daughters who were away at school, because she gave Suzanne, Janice, and myself their bedroom to sleep in while the others slept outside. It seemed strange to be sleeping in a bed with clean sheets in a house with a television on our first night in the Amazon rainforest. I wondered if we were going to find places like this every night.

\*\*\*

In the morning they gave us fresh warm milk from their gentle cow with lovely hot coffee. Bernhardt was impatient to set off and refused to drink the coffee. I got upset with him and told him that not drinking it might mean offending our hosts, but he stubbornly plodded down to the canoe to pout without touching his coffee. The rest of us leisurely enjoyed our cups of their delicious Columbian brew. It was the best coffee I had ever tasted. After working for years on a cruise ship with its regimented routine, I suppose it was hard for Bernhardt to simply go with the flow. Still, I was concerned about Bernhardt's lack of consideration for the local customs and I hoped that in the future his lack of understanding would not cause us problems.

# Chapter 7
# Chiclet on the Putumayo River

*No words to say the way I feel*
*when languages don't meet,*
*yet through the mirage*
*of words we don't have*
*feelings come.*

The Putumayo River is approximately 1,600 km long and is the tenth longest tributary of the Amazon River. It runs from its headwaters in Colombia to Brazil, creating on its way the borders between Colombia, Ecuador, Peru, and Brazil. When the river enters into Brazil, its name changes to Rio Içá. For much of our trip Colombia was on the left shore and another country was on the right shore. A few years after our trip, the Putumayo River became a major cocaine drug route partly because of its remote easy access to so many South American countries.

There were ten of us in our motley international crew, all traveling together in one old dugout canoe. Our indigenous Colombian guide rarely spoke, so Jose soon became the self-proclaimed captain who we called "Captain Pizarro." I had recently been on a canoe trip in Guatemala. I don't think any of the others had much previous canoeing experience. No one, except our guide, knew how to steer the canoe so that was his job.

We were all very naive and young enough to think we knew it all. We didn't even have a map of the area.

When our dugout was purchased, we had neglected to buy enough paddles. It was ridiculous. We had three paddles to use and the guide needed one of them to steer the boat, so only two of us could paddle at a time. We desperately needed to find more paddles, so whenever we passed a shack by the side of the river, we pulled ashore and asked if they had a paddle to sell us. There were no towns and very few people living on the river and those we met did not want to sell us a paddle.

Eventually, we found a man on the Ecuadorian side of the river who was willing to sell us one of his hand-carved paddles. He surprised us with his broad knowledge of world politics which he was excited to talk about with us. I wished that I had a better knowledge of Spanish so that I could understand more of what he said. He lived with his family in an isolated place where a small tributary from Ecuador joined the Putumayo River. On his land grew giant grape trees. I had never seen anything like them before—not vines but huge tall trees, bearing giant bunches of juicy purple grapes. Sergio and Paulo climbed up the trees like agile monkeys and threw grapes down to those of us below. Oh, how delicious they were! We had foolishly not brought any fresh fruit with us to eat. Our generous Ecuadorian host insisted we also take dozens of oranges from his trees with us on our journey. He assured us there were no piranha or caiman in his part of the river, so after filling up on fruit, most of us went for a swim, while Sergio and Jose unsuccessfully tried their hand at fishing.

Our new friend had a little house he had built high up on stilts, with a palm frond roof. He lived here with his wife and three children: a two-week-old baby, a two-year-old boy and a charming five-year-old girl. Unfortunately, the oldest girl was quite physically disabled and could not walk, so she was forced to sit on the raised bamboo floor in the open wooden house all the time. I felt sorry for her. She was a bright and intelligent girl surrounded by the playground of Eden, but was unable to wander through it.

Later in our trip down the river we met more physically and mentally disabled children among the few isolated settlers. I wondered if perhaps with proper medical care, some of these children could have been helped to live normal lives. They were extremely isolated. There were no doctors here. Their only access to the outside world was the river. Could this delightful, little five-year-old have walked if she had been closer to a doctor and received medical care and physical therapy? Not being able to walk here made her extremely vulnerable to parasites and other tropical diseases. As it was, she may have not have survived much longer than a few more years. The jungle is hardest on the weakest.

With our new paddle, we moved on downstream to camp at sunset near a small farm on the Colombia side of the river. We made ourselves a pot of soup for supper. Even though we boiled it, all of us were still nervous about eating it because we had made it from our muddy river's water. Already, we had run out of the drinking water we brought with us. None of us had seriously considered the many potential dangers of the way we were traveling.

Before going to sleep, we swam in what was becoming our brown water lifestream. I jumped into the river first, from a high bank, and as I landed in the murky tributary, I screamed as I felt something enormous in the water beside me. Perhaps I frightened it too, because whatever it was quickly swam away. The inhabitants of this isolated little farm said I was very lucky because there were giant catfish big enough to swallow humans in the water that grew to be twelve feet long and weighed up to 400 pounds. I hastily left the river to sleep by our campfire. Sergio joined me there.

The Amazonian night sky was breathtakingly beautiful. With no electric lights to interfere, the radiant stars took over as they must have since the beginning of time. We spent most of the night watching shooting stars and talked with our eyes, as we didn't yet have a common verbal language. He spoke Portuguese and Spanish, but no English. I spoke no Portuguese and my Spanish was terribly insufficient. On this romantic evening the stars were wonderfully bright. They reflected so brilliantly in the river below that it was difficult to tell the sky apart from the river even as distant lightning occasionally lit up the jungle around us.

\*\*\*

Morning brought us fresh warm milk from the farmer's cows. These isolated river farmers kept the calves away from the mother cows just long enough to be able to milk the cows in the morning to get enough milk for their daily needs. Meanwhile the calves bawled impatiently as they awaited their turn. We packed up our camp, returned everything to the canoe, and were off again. Our food supply of snacks was dwindling rapidly as not one of us had thought to bring real food for the trip. Our heads had been filled with unrealistic fantasies of a jungle paradise filled with abundant fish and tropical fruits free for the picking. We tried to fish again, but were unlucky. The fish jumped all around the canoe, but didn't bite our fishing line. Fortunately, Sergio and Paulo spied some wild peach palm trees on the shore with big clusters of chontaduro fruit. We loaded a bunch of the hard heart-shaped fruit into our canoe and boiled them with salt that evening. They tasted delightfully like roasted chestnuts.

Even though I wore a straw hat all day I still got too much sun. As we pulled into a tiny village called Puerto Ospino, I was feeling faint from heat exhaustion when we were startled by two Columbian police. Upon seeing us arrive they insisted on checking our baggage and passports. I expect we were the most exciting thing that had happened in Puerto Ospino in months. Tired and dirty as we were, we let them check us over. For a moment it looked like the police might find the Brazilians' stash of Columbian weed, but Paulo cleverly gave one of the policemen a Peruvian bead and that satisfactorily deterred them from searching us further.

They actually turned out to be quite nice people and even let us sleep in the police station which, like almost all the structures on the river, was a wooden building on stilts with a palm frond roof. Bernhardt, Robert, and Ditmar were overjoyed because civilized Puerto Ospino had a tiny bar that served cold beer which was chilled through electricity powered by a generator. They got really drunk as we listened to records, drank beer, and danced wildly outside on the jungle floor. We all enjoyed ourselves until the lights suddenly went out along with the music promptly at 9 p.m. In the unexpected sudden darkness, I nearly fell off a cliff into the river as I had been dancing near the water's edge.

Sergio and I started to grow closer. It was strange not speaking the same language. Our common language was Spanish and while we tried to talk, a little something else was communicated without words. It almost seemed better not being able to speak the same language as we were able to avoid the useless nonsensical banter that is so easy to get into with words in a new relationship. A look can communicate more than words. Sergio was a sensitive man and seemed to almost understand my thoughts. I could see new Amazonian sunrises in his eyes. I was falling in love.

As for the rest of our disparate crew, communication continued to be a challenge. Janice, Suzanne, and I spoke English; Sergio and Paulo spoke Portuguese; Bernhardt, Ditmar, and Robert all spoke German. Captain Jose Pizarro and our guide spoke Spanish, but the indigenous guide rarely uttered a word and the rest of us had a pretty poor knowledge of our only common language: Spanish.

*\*\**

Rising early the next day, watching the lazy Putumayo pass by, I wondered what lay ahead. We ate the last of our bread for breakfast, drank coffee, and set off. I was tired even at the beginning of this day.

We paddled on and on in the constant burning sun. At intervals the river shore turned into inviting looking beaches. Janice, Suzanne, and I really wanted to stop, relax, and enjoy the beaches, but our guide, who I was beginning to dislike, said that we had to keep moving. He told us the beaches were too muddy and buggy for us to stop, but actually I believe he was really just in a hurry to get to his home. It made me angry enough to become very bitchy at him and everyone else. The day dragged on. The only food we had left were three oranges from Ecuador.

The Putumayo River was as strange a river as I ever dreamed possible. From nowhere, surfacing, bubbling, swirling masses appeared while giant fish jumped high out of the water to return below, unseen again for the river was a muddy brown and it was impossible to see anything below the surface. At other times the water was so low that we had to get out and push the canoe.

That evening, under an incredibly beautiful sunset sky, we stopped at a tiny one-room schoolhouse for the night. Hot and exhausted, I immediately jumped into the river, which, on the surface, appeared to have no current, but as soon as I entered the water, I realized how deceiving it had been. Even though I was swimming as fast as I possibly could against the current, I was still being carried downstream and away from the shore quickly. My canoe-mates laughed, thinking I was being funny. I panicked, swimming, kicking, and splashing. Sergio realized that I was in real trouble and reached out with a strong arm to grab me before I was carried away down the brown river into darkness. He saved my life!

On the way up the steep hill from the river to the little schoolhouse, our guide accidentally stepped with his hard boot on my bare foot. It hurt like hell. I was able to forget about my pain and hunger soon though, when some friendly, curious women who lived near the schoolhouse cooked us some chicken and rice to eat. After dinner I heard the simple, clear sound of a bamboo flute in the darkness. My head began to spin with the magic of the music. I danced with my socks on, as I was afraid of stepping on a snake in the dark, wet, cool grass. I don't know why I thought socks would protect me from a snakebite. Fortunately, my impromptu dancing did not attract any reptiles. When the flute music finished, I saw that the player had been Sergio—my dancing unseen by him.

The night was lovely and cool. We were surrounded by the enchanting calls of frogs and other rainforest creatures. Some of us slept outside in the grass under the open sky, until rain poured down upon us in the middle of the night. We grabbed our sleeping bags and ran madly in the darkness to reach the dry shelter of the old wooden schoolhouse. This was the first rain they had had in months and a sign that the dry season was drawing to a close.

*** 

Walking back down to the canoe in the morning was an extremely muddy affair after the torrential rainstorm the night before. My foot was now swollen and hurting again, but I had much more energy after the refreshing cool night rain. We paddled on steadily without stopping until about noon when we reached a settlement in Peru and realized that we had just paddled across the equator. For our first equator-crossing initiation, Janice, Suzanne, and I were all thrown into the river to prove that we were worthy of making the transition. We were now considered to be daughters of Neptune. It was wonderful fun. I could hardly believe I had just crossed the equator. Of course, the equator can't be seen, but somehow, I could sense it and feel its effects. It was exhilarating to know I had actually paddled across the middle of the earth.

We arrived at a Peruvian settlement that was one of the bigger places we had passed since leaving Puerto Asis. We ate lunch in the little town's only restaurant, but poor Suzanne couldn't stomach the food as she was now suffering from a bad case of diarrhea. After a delicious meal of yucca and fish soup, Sergio and I wandered off on our own to observe the village. It was on this walk that Sergio first told me he had feelings for me.

*Janice, Jose, and Robert waiting at the dugout canoe.*

When we eventually returned to our canoe everyone else was angry at us and impatiently waiting in the canoe ready to leave. I couldn't understand what the hurry was. Here we were on the Amazon in a dugout canoe, explorers journeying into the unknown and they wanted to rush. The Europeans were in a particular hurry. After this incident and others like it, I began to dislike them more and more. Bernhardt expressed his anger by paddling so fast with such energy he earned the nickname "Motorboat."

We hadn't gone far when our dugout canoe began to leak. We had nothing to patch the crack in her side. The guide had nothing either, so I came up with the brilliant idea of using the Chiclet chewing gum that I had stored in my backpack. It worked surprisingly well at stopping the leak. Suzanne had previously wanted to name our dugout "Huckleberry Finn," but we Canadians were the only ones in the crew who had read Mark Twain's writings so that wasn't popular. I had liked the name "African Queen" but our dugout really was closer to a raft than a boat with an engine. Everyone had heard of Chiclets and they saved the day, so our dugout canoe was immediately christened "Chiclet."

*** 

As each day passed, the temperature became hotter, the jungle vines on the shoreline became denser, while signs of human life became scarcer. Just before sunset, we were relieved to see a small shack by the edge of the water.

*Robert and Alycin paddling their dugout canoe, Chiclet,*
*on the Putumayo River.*

Pulling into shore we asked if we might spend the night there. A man, a woman, and a boy of about sixteen lived here. When the boy moved, I noticed that he had a club foot and appeared to be mentally challenged. These people didn't talk. They just stared at us while the man nodded his head. Later, the small quiet woman made us some chicken soup. While she cooked, I looked around the house. The boy sat in a corner staring strangely at us while he quietly cuddled a small capuchin monkey. I suppose he had never seen anything like us before.

In the kitchen at the back of the two-room house were two baby parrots in a nest. I couldn't quite make out what the people who lived here were thinking about us. They were completely silent. When the soup was finally ready and all of us were served, Ditmar let out a loud, horrifying scream. He had the chicken's head staring up at him in his soup, beak and all. The rest of us roared with laughter, but not wanting to offend the cook, I thanked her heartily for my portion of the soup which luckily didn't have a chicken head in it. Robert got the feet but politely said nothing.

*Alycin and Sergio setting up her tent by the Putumayo River.*

As I crawled into my tent to sleep that night, I noticed several bites on my stomach. Nobody seemed to know what they were. My foot that the guide had stepped on was really starting to hurt again so Janice kindly gave me a foot massage. Paulo, Suzanne, Janice, Sergio, and I all slept in my small nylon pup tent together that night as it was pouring with rain. Sergio and I cuddled together as did Paulo and Suzanne. Poor Janice slept uncomfortably alone in the middle. I was the only one of our crew who had brought a tent. The rest of our crew slept outside under palm leaf canopies in hammocks.

Before the rain came down, we had a phenomenal bonfire. Our lanky Swiss crewmate Ditmar went absolutely insane. He ran screaming into the rainforest with a machete and returned numerous times with enormous branches for the fire, breaking them into pieces in front of us with his bare hands. He was frightening. The only thing that cooled his frenetic behavior and stopped him from continuing his jungle madness was a downpour of rain. Ditmar was an unusually strange man, deathly afraid to talk to women and a giant among men, being at least a foot taller than anyone else in our crew. During the trip he became seriously sunburnt. His hands and face swelled up like overripe tomatoes. That night must have been real torture for him because it was the first night that we had encountered mosquitoes. They could bite through anything. There is nothing worse than a mosquito bite on sunburnt skin. Only those of us in the tent were safe from them. Thank goodness I had been traveling with my tent.

\*\*\*

Strangely, the next morning I had twice as many bites on my stomach as I had the night before. These were not mosquito bites. I was truly beginning to get worried as they were not only multiplying rapidly, they were also driving me crazy because I couldn't stop scratching them. My injured foot was now swollen to the extent that it was difficult to walk. I was glad we were traveling by canoe and not by foot. Everyone was tired. Not only that, but our very meager food supply had been raided the night before by insects so that all of it had to be thrown away. We didn't eat anything for breakfast or lunch. As we traveled along, we kept our eyes out for any kind of jungle fruit that might be growing on shore.

One of our four paddles was much rougher and heavier than the others. It functioned as a method of propulsion, but was definitely much more work to use than any of the others and consequently not popular. Out of the blue, for no apparent reason, Captain Jose Pizarro suddenly threw the heavy paddle into the middle of the river. We were all so completely shocked by his impulsive action that the entire crew sat silently, mouths agape, for a moment and watched it float away downstream. Granted, the paddle had been heavy, but my God, we now had a huge canoe in the middle of nowhere and only three paddles.

Not knowing what else to say I screamed at Jose, "That certainly was a selfish thing to do!"

He just smiled.

We paddled on and on, hungry and tired. We had started that morning and continued on until noon without a break. Suzanne had developed dysentery and was desperate to stop and let loose. Janice and I had to pee, but our guide at the helm refused to stop our canoe. He just went on saying that there was a much prettier place ahead to go ashore. He continued on this way for at least an hour. We were all about to die. Eventually he guided "Chiclet" to land. Janice, Suzanne, and I all raced out and immediately did our business on the shore without even looking for a bush to hide behind. I was furious. He could stand up and pee over the side of the canoe anytime. For a man that was easy, but for a woman it was almost impossible. He was torturing us with his little macho game in the middle of the Amazon rainforest. I couldn't believe it. The spot he picked to come ashore didn't even have anything we could harvest to eat. We were all very hungry.

A few hours downstream we were overjoyed to see a large grove of wild guava trees loaded with fruit. We immediately jumped out and climbed the trees like monkeys eating the fruit as we filled our hats and pockets with fruit to take with us. Barely had we returned to the water in our canoe when Paulo started to scream bloody murder in Portuguese and dove into the river. It turned out that he had unknowingly climbed a guava tree that was also home to giant, biting, black ants. They didn't start to bite him until after he was in the canoe. Thinking of his bites I noticed that my bites were spreading all over my body. In the center of each bite was a tiny yellow spot. This strange affliction was beginning to frighten me.

From what our guide said, it appeared that we might arrive in Leguizamo later that day, that is, if we paddled hard all day. And so, without food and only three paddles, we went on.

The river widened out into a large lake. The shortest way across the lake was through the middle. As we reached a point very far from shore, suddenly from out of nowhere came a great blast of wind. What had been a tranquil placid lake had now turned dangerously rough. It became necessary to paddle with all of our strength into the white caps just to keep Chiclet from overturning.

For several hours we fought against the elements when just as suddenly as it had come up, the wind disappeared. Exhausted, almost ready to give up, we continued, with the going much easier now the wind had stopped. I wondered if we would ever get to this town or whatever it was we were headed toward.

*Exhausted, Janice, Captain Jose Pizzaro,
and Alycin in Chiclet.*

*Sergio resting on the front of Chiclet in the Putumayo River.*

# Chapter 8
# *Some Fly Away*

### *Slaughter in Leguizamo*

*Quiet cow beast trembling in the dirt,*

*Falling, struggling against human ropes,*

*with your last crying breath of life.*

*Your death means nothing; No one cares.*

*Your unborn children, are unborn,*

*Your companions in the slaughter yard*

*think only of themselves.*

*While some human mouth will complain because*

*you are too old and tough.*

In the distance behind us, we heard the out of place sound of an engine. It came closer and closer until a small boat with a motor pulled up beside us. To our great surprise, Christian, the Frenchman we had left behind in Puerto Asis, was in the boat. He stood up, smiled, and waved at us like passing royalty as he motored on ahead. We all stopped paddling and stared at him in amazement until the sound of his engine had almost disappeared and he was gone.

With no other option we paddled on and on again until we began to notice there were several shacks on the Columbian side of the river. Children appeared waving and smiling as they adeptly maneuvered their small dugout canoes near to us. Our guide gave out a joyous cry: "Leguizamo!"

*Puerto Leguizamo, Colombia.*

I looked ahead, but all I could see were wooden shacks on the left side of the river and a gloating Christian standing waiting on the shore.

Puerto Leguizamo, Colombia, was a small town with one main street. It was the biggest place we had seen so far in our adventure. Its claim to fame was a small dirt landing strip for airplanes on the far edge of town. We walked into town looking for a place to stay. I saw a crowd of people on one side of the street and went over to see what was happening. A poor old cow was being brutally slaughtered on the side of the road. We moved on.

Paulo, Suzanne, Janice, Sergio, and I checked into what was the only place to stay: Hotel Putumayo. It had a few small dirty rooms in the back and a tiny restaurant with two tables out front. The five of us shared one room for ten pesos each a night. The rest of the crew took the other rooms. Luckily, Hotel Putumayo had running water and a shower. Granted, the shower only had cold water, still this was the most civilization we had seen since the start of our canoe trip. The weather was so hot and humid, a cold shower was actually quite enjoyable.

On our first evening in town after washing off the sweat and dirt from our travels, we dressed up. We had been wearing our "jungle shirts" every day for way too long. It is hard to dress up when you have been living out of a backpack for months with just a few practical pieces of clothing, so we exchanged clothes. I wore Janice's skirt with my Guatemalan embroidered top. Janice wore Suzanne's dress and Suzanne wore my skirt and turned Paulo's green handkerchief into a cute top. She was a clever seamstress. We had a wonderful evening and took a picture to remember it.

I learned from the hotel owner that my itchy bumps were not a rash at all, but tiny, multiplying, biting, yellow spiders who were making homes in my skin. I was forced to use a sewing needle to tediously stab each tiny spider to remove it. Sergio helped me as I could not reach all of them. I felt much better when most of them were gone and I swore to never lie in the grass again because that is how they got to me. They reminded me of the chiggers that burrow under your skin when you sit in the grass or touch fallen Spanish Moss in the southern United States.

*Paulo, Suzanne, Janice, Alycin, and Sergio dressed up for fun in Puerto Leguizamo, Colombia.*

\*\*\*

It turned out that the next day a cargo plane was leaving from the landing strip to fly to an airport near Bogotá. It was a small plane with a questionable cargo of several big kerosene oil drums inside it. The plane only seated six—including the pilot. There was only one flight a week so there was room for only five of us to go. Bernhardt, Robert, and Ditmar were insistent they be on the plane. They could not take any more of the physical hardships and culture shocks of canoe life. Janice decided to go too because she was afraid that Chiclet was not going to get us to Brazil in time to meet her sister and mother in Rio. Suzanne had been traveling with Janice since Canada so she kissed Paulo goodbye, promising to meet him later in Brazil and we watched as five of our crew abandoned ship and flew away.

There wasn't room for me and I was not prepared to desert Chiclet. I was still eager to explore more of the Amazon Basin and get to know Sergio better in the process. The river was choosing its wanderers. The realities of the sweltering humid heat, insects, disease, and other dangers were not something everyone voluntarily chose to embrace. Our mysterious Putumayo River still called to me.

We considered selling Chiclet and getting a barge to Leticia until we learned it could be another month before one could get up the river, so it was decided that Sergio, Paulo, Jose, and I continue our adventure in Chiclet. Our "old friend" Christian and a French couple, Pedro and Isabela, decided to join us too as they had also found themselves stranded in Puerto Leguizamo. Isabela was a beautiful, dark-haired woman and her partner, fair-haired Pedro, seemed to be a pleasant, easygoing man. Neither of them spoke much English. We were all young dreamers living in a fantasy world. What lay ahead we did not know. I was a little afraid, not so much of the river, but more of the strange combination of people who were going to travel together on the incredible journey ahead of us. We were bound to be both amazed and disillusioned by what lay ahead. I wondered what was going to happen if our dreams fell apart and we were left with the hard, bitter truths of the rainforest. I still had a mild skin infection and my sprained foot hurt so much I wondered if it was broken, but nothing could stop me from embarking on this adventure.

\*\*\*

Christian awakened all of us the next morning at 7:00 a.m. by shouting it was time to go. He had already packed up his gear which included French law books as he planned to ultimately return to France and become an attorney. Jose and Christian started their day arguing about money and the past wars between France and Spain! I was beginning to dread the thought of traveling with both of them in the same canoe. This time we packed some real food for the trip. We had purchased a large bag of bread, some dry rice, and beans. Jose and Christian argued over how much food to bring. They were always arguing. Christian decided to also purchase some onions, spaghetti, and spices. There really was not anything else available to buy in this town, so we set out at 3:30 p.m. with our guide steering in the back of the canoe.

Our guide was surprisingly more cheerful than he had been the entire trip. We took this to be a good omen. However, after we had paddled for nearly two more days, he gleefully pointed out a small house on the Colombian shore and shouted, "Esa es mi casa!" (That's my house!)

It seemed fair that we should stop at his home for the night.

\*\*\*

The next morning when we were ready to leave, we could not find him. Eventually, Jose and Christian found him only to be told that he was quitting as our guide. We were on our own.

This was a frightening prospect. The Putumayo River was completely unpredictable. From one day to the next, the water level rose and fell by several feet. This part of the Putumayo was hardly populated at all and it was getting less and less so. Since Puerto Leguizamo we had only passed two small houses.

We demanded that he, at least, take us to a place where there was a motorboat. He reluctantly agreed and took us a short way downstream to where he showed us a rusty old motor on a boat that had been dragged high up onto the shore. We smiled with relief, until we realized that he had disappeared and there was no gasoline for the engine. The engine was completely useless without gasoline. Jose and Christian began to argue again. Christian argued about everything. His mouth never stopped.

With no other choice, we returned to Chiclet and continued our journey without a guide. Jose and Christian both considered themselves the captain of our expedition and took turns at the stern while the rest of us continued the arduous chore of paddling. We knew, or at least hoped, that if we kept going downstream and took the correct forks in the river, we should eventually come to the Amazon River and Leticia where we were sure we could catch a boat to Brazil. It was still not the rainy season, but unlike the Putumayo River, the huge Amazon River always has plenty of water in it for big boats to travel on year round. Unfortunately, we had absolutely no idea of how far it was or how long it was going to take us to get there.

We found a small farm to camp at that night. The inhabitants generously gave us plantain and fish to eat so we cooked our food over an open fire. These nights on the river were enchantingly beautiful. The silver moon floated magically above us in the gathering mist. I was grateful that I had my old faithful blue nylon tent with me. It was my sanctuary away from the nightly mosquitoes and during the deepest, most frightening jungle nights I felt safe and at home inside it. Sergio shared the tent with me while everyone else slept outside in their hammocks tied to trees.

\*\*\*

I was the first one up the next day. I listened, mesmerized by the calls of colorful, exotic birds as I watched a breathtaking sunrise. When I left my tent to start breakfast, I noticed that our camp was a torn-up mess. Amazonian wild pigs called peccaries had silently raided our camp in the night. Luckily, I had placed most of our food up high hanging from a rope on a tree so it was safe, but the pigs had eaten all of our coffee. Peccaries look like hairy wild pigs, but genetically they are a different species. They live in herds of 20 to 200 and can range over a territory as large as 100 miles. They are omnivores and live mostly on fruits, nuts, grasses, and small animal meat when they can catch it. I expect this was their first taste of coffee. I wasn't much of a coffee drinker, but the rest of the crew became quite irritable when they realized there would be no more morning coffee to drink.

Thinking I would start my day with a swim instead, I stopped in my tracks when I saw a large Black Caiman submerged near where our canoe was tied. Black Caiman are an Amazonian crocodilian. They tend to stick to shallow waters and can grow to be thirteen feet in length. Some have been reported to be nearly twenty feet long, making it one of the largest caiman species in South America. Adult Black Caiman typically feed on fish, but have also been known to snatch capybaras, deer, peccaries, and even people from the banks of the river. The Black Caiman is now listed as an endangered species; however, it was still quite abundant in this part of the river then. This was the first caiman I had ever seen. Hastily, I decided to not have a morning swim.

Later that day, we passed through an extremely dense area of rainforest. At one point ahead of us we saw a single canoe. It appeared to contain two dark-haired people, one in front and one at the back. As we drew closer, we could see there was also a small child in the middle. Their canoe moved with such ease it seemed to be flying across the water. All three were naked, with long dark hair hanging around their shoulders, but before our heavy dugout could get close enough to communicate with them, they were gone, disappearing into the vast undergrowth on a narrow side stream. The entire crew remained fairly quiet the rest of the day. We watched and listened to the sounds of the river moving along against the overgrown, green tropical shoreline knowing that we had now entered an unfamiliar world.

*\*\**

We continued on, stopping every night at dusk, whenever we could find a place on shore with room enough to set up a tent—which was rare. We sometimes went days without seeing any people. There were no more houses on either shore nor any signs of human life. We were alone in the deep, overpowering, primordial realm of the rainforest. Days passed as we paddled down the wide, slow-moving, shallow river. Every once in a while, we saw a large caiman resting on the shore watching us. They didn't move. They just watched us pass by.

When one is surrounded by nothing but the green beauty of the jungle for days on end, a kind of madness sneaks into one's mind. It affects everyone differently. Pedro seemed to be affected the most. One day the wind was blowing against us and we had to paddle very hard just to keep going forward. Paddling all day long was both exhausting and boring. There was no use complaining. There was nothing else for us to do.

Still, Pedro complained bitterly, until we reached a section of the river where the water was quite deep and he belligerently announced, "I'm not in this anymore," and jumped out of the canoe into the water.

We were stunned. Isabela, his girlfriend, was speechless. The water looked calm, but this was one of the tricks of the Putumayo River. An undercurrent like the one that had almost pulled me away earlier in the trip grabbed Pedro and before we knew what was happening, his blond, bobbing head had disappeared downstream out of sight! He was gone. I feared we were never going to see him again.

We paddled after him as fast as we could. The wind became so strong that it actually blew us upstream in the opposite direction. Our homemade tarp shade canopy in the middle of the canoe was acting like a sail, until it blew off completely and we were blown with it to the opposite shore.

It seemed like hours had passed when we finally found Pedro clinging onto an overhanging branch in the river. We had to fight the wind to get to him. The current was so strong, that Christian at the stern snapped his rudder paddle in half in the process. Finally, we managed to maneuver our canoe to reach Pedro. Everyone was angry with him. Sergio, Jose, and Christian yelled loud enough to scare away all the animals in the jungle. As the men raged at Pedro, I peered cautiously into the frightening, green paradise that surrounded us. We were on the brink of something incredible while they were caught up in anger.

As we set off again down the river, everyone, but me, smoked a cigarette to calm down from the previous hectic few hours. I had never been a smoker. Instead, I got into the Zen of paddling to calm down. On every side, the rainforest grew denser with giant trees covered with tangles of reaching vines. There was no place to dock our canoe. I wondered if we were ever going to find a place to camp for the night. We finally decided to stop at one of the many beautiful beaches that we came upon. Previously, our guide had stubbornly refused to allow us to land on any sandbars. Just as we started to set up camp, the sand began to disappear under water. The water rose surprisingly quickly. We barely had time to get our gear back into Chiclet. One does not think of inland rivers as having tides, but the Putumayo had mysterious current-like tides. The river was telling us to move on.

*The shoreline along the Putumayo River was so dense it was rarely possible to land.*

*One of the infrequent tiny farms that we passed on the Putumayo River.*

# Chapter 9
# Caiman and Pink Dolphins in Peru

*Turn on the wheels of a wilderness*
*our forefathers destroyed,*
*Fall beneath the leaves of emerald trees*
*resting in the sands of time*
*where caimans bite*
*our heroes of the dark Putumayo*

It is almost impossible to explain how it feels to be lost in the middle of nowhere with no end in sight. Dawn began with the morning songs of exotic wild birds as the sun peeked over our lifeline: the muddy Putumayo River. We ate a meager breakfast of leftovers from supper the night before and set out in our leaky dugout canoe, each taking turns paddling until we became too tired. Exhausted and wondering if we were ever going to find an end to this river adventure, we were rewarded when loud calls from above revealed a brilliantly colored, large flock of red-tailed scarlet macaw parrots flying overhead. Their joyous freedom in flight was contagious. They inspired us to continue on through this everchanging dangerous green wilderness.

As the day neared an end, we came to a place that had enough cleared land to camp on, but Captain Jose Pizarro, who was now at the stern, imagining himself a Spanish conquistador, insisted it wasn't good enough. He steered us downriver past some tall trees announcing, "There is a better place to camp a little further on."

The rest of us were ready to stop, but too tired to argue with him. We rounded the next bend in the river and looked ahead to see nothing but dense rainforest.

*Nothing but dense rainforest for miles and miles.*

Resting on the narrow shoreline beneath the dropping tangle of vines, we saw several young Black Caiman, no more than two feet long, lying in wait for prey. I looked down at the muddy water below us and imagined all of the larger caiman we couldn't see, waiting and watching our rotting Chiclet canoe pass by. To make matters worse, Jose began to talk about hunting crocodiles that night because their skins were worth so much money.

We continued on until we found ourselves in a narrow, calm, very shallow part of the river where our dugout canoe got stuck, truly stuck. Chiclet refused to move an inch until everyone got out of the canoe to push her across the big sandbar we were trapped on. The river shore was now lined on both sides with several big ten-foot-long, hungry looking Black Caiman watching us. Knowing that Black Caiman have excellent sight and can travel thirty miles an hour in water, I did not want to get out, but had no choice. I was the last one to leave the safety of our canoe because I was terrified. Bravely, we pushed and shoved until we finally moved Chiclet into deeper, murky water. I don't know how we made it out of there alive, but somehow, we did. Perhaps we were too many and too loud for the silent, staring reptiles to dare attack us. Jose didn't talk about crocodile hunting again.

We were exhausted. As the sun was about to set, we heard screams and the loud voices of people. *Was someone having a party by the river?* Ahead of us, on the Peruvian shore, we saw a tiny bamboo hut so we pulled in, tied up Chiclet, and climbed up the hill to the hut. We were met by a man with a frightening grin waving a bloody machete. There was blood everywhere. Terrified, I was sure he was going to murder us, but instead, it turned out that he was smiling because he had just killed a huge capybara. The "party" screams we had heard were the cries of the poor animal being slaughtered. His wife and two children watched us approach as they prepared a fire to cook the animal.

Capybara are the world's largest rodents. Adults can weigh over 100 pounds and grow to be four feet long and two feet tall. Their webbed feet make them excellent swimmers.

These cute herbivores look very much like giant cousins of the guinea pig. I felt sorry for the poor creature.

After each savage slaughter I witnessed on the river, I became more and more sure I should return to being a vegetarian. I had been a vegetarian after my travels in India a few years before and had only started eating meat again while traveling in Central America, because it was the food that was offered to me, and to refuse it would have been an insult. I wondered how humans could be so inhumane. In the jungle, hunting was part of survival, but the killing didn't have to be done in such a brutal, cruel way.

The man with the machete told us about a larger farm a little further on. His bit of cleared land by his hut was so small there was not even room enough to put up a pup tent. We set off again. Exhausted as we were, I was glad we were leaving his blood-stained plot. We zigzagged slowly down the river. I was so tired I could hardly lift my paddle. It was almost dark when we came to the next little farm. Mercifully, it was a larger piece of land and had just enough room to camp. I quickly pitched my tent under some banana trees and went down to the river to bathe. Paulo caught a large fish and proceeded to make a campfire to cook it. I went back to my tent and passed out for a few hours until I was awakened by Sergio to come eat supper. I was too tired to eat. From my tent I watched a bright moon rise behind our jungle cooking fire. The evening mosquitoes were out now, driving everyone to take cover. Still, the incredible beauty of the rainforest eliminated the hardships for me and made it all worthwhile.

\*\*\*

The next morning, I looked out my tent to find a tiny pygmy marmoset monkey peering curiously in at me. We watched each other for a moment before it slowly crawled away. Jose and Christian had started a fire. I arrived just in time to hear their argument about which was better: cafe or cafe con leche. I could not understand why on this beautiful morning they were wasting energy arguing about something so trivial. We didn't even have any coffee left! Everyone was in a poor mood that morning, but after breakfast, a joint of Colombian grass was passed around and we all started to cheer up. Sergio played his flute and we were off again. It was my turn to take a paddle. I relished the work under the warm sun paddling through the foamy brown waters of our river.

We stopped for lunch at a beautiful well-made little bamboo house on the river and talked with the man who lived there. He was a handsome, charming man who had fourteen children. His sweet kind wife lit a fire for us to cook on. How did our ungrateful crew respond? We argued about who was going to cook lunch. The fire was already lit so Jose and I started to make lunch, but we didn't really want to do it. It was incredibly hot cooking by the fire in the middle of the day and I had cooked lunch the day before. Another argument ensued about cooking in the future. It was ridiculous. I was angry that we were fighting in front of these friendly people's innocent children. Then I lost my mind and screamed uncontrollably like a mad woman. When I finally finished my out-of-control tirade, I wanted to cry or die of embarrassment and sadness. I was ashamed of myself. This was not my dream adventure. I wished I was not in a canoe with these crazy people. We left quickly after eating lunch and paddled on.

*** 

We had not seen any people for several days when we were happily surprised to see a woman with long black hair on a sandbar making something. Her open mouth at the sight of us quickly turned into a smile. She generously offered us a drink of the concoction she was brewing. It was an alcoholic beverage and tasted quite horrid. She didn't speak Spanish so we could not communicate with words. We guessed she must speak some native tongue so we smiled with gratitude as we bravely sipped her offering.

We had not been there long when a man with short black hair arrived. He was not friendly. He started shouting in a language none of us could understand, however his message was clear. He wanted us to leave. He was very angry and made threatening moves with his fists. We left as quickly as we could. When I looked back, I saw him hitting the woman with a log. She cowered from his attack as we rounded a bend in the river. I desperately wanted to go back to help her. She had been very kind to us, but the others thought it unsafe for us to do so. They feared there might be other men hidden in the surrounding rainforest that would attack us if we went back. So we left the poor woman to her fate and paddled on. Her screams echoed behind us.

As we floated along in the canoe, Sergio, Paulo, and Jose took turns with a fishing line and in this part of the river, unlike earlier in the trip, they were quite successful. In fact, just about every time they threw in a fishing line, they caught a fish: a piranha. Piranha are bony, but they are quite good fried in oil, especially when you don't have anything else to eat. We ate a few at night whenever we caught some. Even though we knew there were piranha, it was so unbearably hot and humid that we continued to swim in the river each evening to cool off. Fortunately, the piranha were not attracted to us. Contrary to popular belief, piranha rarely attack unless there are exceptional circumstances. Most piranha are actually more inclined to feed like vultures on the weak or dead animals they find in the water, usually only attacking when they smell blood.

Then the rains came. At first, the rain was refreshingly cool, but then it came down harder and harder for hours. One of us had to constantly bail water out of Chiclet to keep our canoe from filling with water.

During one torrential downpour, we saw a strange, intense, persistent splashing in the river up ahead. Curious, we moved our canoe closer to see that the commotion in the water was created by a huge dead fish being attacked by hundreds of small piranhas. Fascinated by the piranhas' activity, we tied a rope around the tail of the dead fish and pulled it alongside our canoe. The fish must have weighed at least 100 pounds. It was still pouring down with rain. Then Paulo went crazy. It was as if he had become one with the shoal of piranha. He began attacking the big dead fish with a knife, stabbing at it frantically until he dropped his knife in the water. Even without the knife, he continued attacking the dead fish with his bare fists. The rain was coming down so heavily now it was like canoeing through a waterfall. We had to stop or our canoe was going to fill with water and sink, so we pulled to shore on the Peruvian side and let our dead monster fish float away with its hungry entourage, while we climbed soaking wet onto the muddy shore. As the fish disappeared, Paulo calmed down, returned to himself, and recovered from his moment of jungle madness. It rained all that night and was so cold I needed to wear a sweater.

*\*\*\**

Another day, we saw a few canoes tied up by the shore to a small dock. Thinking this might be a great place to rest and find out more about where we were, we happily turned Chiclet toward the shore. As we approached the dock, two men came running out waving their arms and shouting at us. I didn't understand exactly what they were saying, but I did understand that they didn't want us to get out of our canoe. We were exhausted and needed a rest place to stop so I ignored them and kept paddling toward the shore. Captain Jose Pizarro, who was positioned at the stern of the canoe, shouted, "Stop paddling, Alycin! Stop!" He understood what the men were saying. Earlier that day a man who had been standing in the water by the dock had been killed by an electric eel. The Amazonian electric eel can grow to be eight feet long, and when hunting or defending itself can send out a shock of 850 volts. The men shouting on the shore were not unfriendly; they were trying to save our lives! We continued on.

This event reminded me of a small tribe of indigenous people I had read about called the Matis in Brazilian Amazon. They were renowned for their ability to hunt electric eels. Before hunting, they performed a ceremony that involved putting small amounts of Poison Arrow Frogs' toxic secretions under the hunter's skin like a tattoo. The hunter then amazingly was able to corner an electric eel in shallow water during the dry season and actually pick it up with his bare hands without being hurt by the eel's tremendous electric shock. No one understands how they can do this. There is so much we don't know and could learn from the original peoples of this rainforest, if we only respected their way of life and protected their wild territories.

The Putumayo River in the dry season is a tediously slow, snakelike winding river. Consequently, the distance we had roughly estimated traveling when we started out on this trip was much further than we had ever imagined. Not surprisingly, we were running out of food. Daily, we scanned the shoreline for fruit-bearing trees at each new bend in the river. Eventually we saw a large grove of wild banana trees growing on the riverside. Overjoyed, Sergio, Paulo, and Jose eagerly rushed into the banana grove with their machetes to cut down a bunch of bananas for us to eat. Jose, in his excitement, cut his hand quite severely with his machete. We were able to eventually stop the bleeding and bandage his hand, but infection soon set in. To make matters worse, the bananas were all still too green to eat.

***

We went several more days without seeing anyone or finding any wild food to forage for on the impenetrable shore. The river often forked with two or more channels, and without a guide or a map, we had to guess which way to go, hoping the channel we chose would take us downstream and not to a dead end.

Our trip was seemingly endless when suddenly, out of nowhere, like a miracle, a pod of pink river dolphins surrounded our canoe. It had been my dream to find these rare

Amazonian dolphins. They had found me! I was overjoyed. The Amazon River dolphin, also known as the pink river dolphin, is found exclusively in the Amazon Basin. They are the only dolphin that lives in freshwater. When these dolphins get excited, they can flush a bright pink, similar to humans blushing. Our beautiful dolphins were flamingo pink.

We watched them gleefully jump and play around Chiclet, until they made a pattern in front of us and we understood that we were meant to follow them. The dolphins were our new guides. They led us into a tributary that parted from the main river. We followed our dolphins silently as if in a magical dream upstream on this new river for close to an hour. When we came to a bend in the river, our dolphins became excited and called out to each other splashing and jumping out of the water. Mesmerized, we watched them frolic, until we became aware of a man with long black hair intently staring at us from the shore.

# Chapter 10
# The Mythical Realm of the Dolphin Tribe

**"Many wise people say that animals do not understand, but animals do not go around ruining nature so we think that animals do understand and that people have much to learn from them."—words of a shaman.**

The pink river dolphins had alerted the man on the shore to our presence. He was quickly joined by the rest of his tribe which included men, women, and children. They were all barefoot and had the same clear dark eyes with long, straight, black hair. The men wore long tunic-like dresses. The women wore colorful skirts with little capes and were otherwise topless. Their capes were worn to the back most of the time and in front when they were holding or nursing their babies. Most of the children were naked. They all smiled and greeted us with outreached hands, encouraging us to bring our canoe to shore where several of their own small dugout canoes were docked.

We brought Chiclet to land and followed the tribe into a large communal bamboo house on stilts, with a woven palm frond roof. I was immediately impressed by how clean and well-made this house was compared to the many houses we had seen previously on our trip down the Putumayo. Their roof was not just laid with dried palm leaves, but instead with intricately woven palm leaves made into an impeccably thatched waterproof roof. Elaborately handmade string hammocks were hung all around inside the house circling a small cooking fire in the middle. They invited us to come sit around their fire and a few of them casually climbed into their hammocks to watch us. One woman held a woolly monkey in her arms and some of the children played with a pair of green parrots that were perched inside the house. After I sat down, several of the women from the tribe came up to me and gently touched my hair. I don't think they had ever seen blonde hair before. Paulo was quite a hairy man, especially compared to the indigenous men who didn't have any facial hair. The woman crowded around Paulo as well and touched his beard.

These gentle, friendly people had never seen anything like us. They were as fascinated by us as we were by them. They gave us an orange tasting beverage to drink that was delicious, and cooked some plantain on the fire for us to eat. They encouraged us to try out their beautiful hammocks. They were the most comfortable hammocks I had ever been in.

In an odd gesture of friendship, Christian handed out cigars to the men who were sitting around the fire with us. As he passed cigars to the men, a woman reached forward to take one too. Being European, he had not expected the women to want a cigar, but with a smile gave her one. They studied the cigars carefully and smelled them. Christian then lit the cigars and they all smoked. I thought it was a very inappropriate gesture, but these indigenous people liked it and smiled. Pedro offered the chief an American dollar bill in exchange for a hammock. The whole tribe studied the money. I was silently furious with Pedro for offering them such a small amount for a hammock that had obviously taken many weeks to make. I quietly told him he should give them more. He ignored me. It reminded me of the early Europeans in America who bought land from the natives with colorful beads.

The tribe then took us back down to the river and indicated we should follow one of them in a canoe further upstream, which we did. We left the women and children playing and bathing naked in their clear river. A member of their tribe fishing from a small dugout canoe waved at us as we passed. A little further on we saw a section of land that had been burned to clear it for planting. New green shoots of banana plants were already starting to grow up. The further we went upstream, the clearer the river water became. We had not paddled far when we came upon another indigenous village with several more communal bamboo buildings thatched with woven palm leaf roofs. Again, we were greeted by friendly people dressed in similar clothing and much to our surprise, a young white woman named Ana. The villagers each reached out—not to shake—but to touch our hands, as this was apparently their custom. We touched hands with every member of the tribe.

Ana, who spoke English, introduced herself as a French woman who had been staying with this Secoya tribe, or the Siekopa'ai as they called themselves, to study them here on the Yubineto River. She was glad to see us too. We had not been there long when we heard the sound of an engine. A Peruvian policeman arrived in a motorized dugout canoe. He told us we could not be there without a permit and we had to leave. I tried to explain in my broken Spanish that the pink dolphins had brought us here so we belonged. He ignored me and insisted we get back into our canoe and follow him. Ana told us that there was a Peruvian police border outpost not too far away near the mouth of the Yubineto River where it joined with the Putumayo River and that he wanted us to follow him there.

I was extremely disappointed. I wanted to stay with the tribe to learn more about their way of life, spiritual wisdom, and rainforest skills. I had studied medical herbal uses in Canada and learned more about rainforest herbs from the family I had stayed with in the mountains of Costa Rica. Secoya tribes were known to have a deep knowledge of medicinal herbs, with traditional uses for over 1000 different plants. Our dolphin guides had brought us to one of the last remaining indigenous tribes with this ancient knowledge. For thousands of years, their ancestors had understood and cared for our planet's largest rainforest.

Just over a century ago, many of the indigenous peoples in this area of the Amazon Basin were almost completely decimated by the rubber boom that was fueled by the insatiable hunger of our industrial world, for the crucial raw material from the rubber tree that kept our cars and machines running. Indigenous people were perceived as inferior beings. They were captured and brutally forced to work in the jungle to harvest the white rubber tree sap. It is believed that at least 100,000 died. They were enslaved, murdered, their communities destroyed, their women raped, and their children killed or left orphans by the cruel slave owners who had the power to get rid of anyone who dared question their authority. Somehow this tribe had survived and retained its unique culture and of love of the rainforest where they lived.

Unenthusiastically, we returned to Chiclet and paddled slowly away. I waved goodbye to the people I now refer to as the Dolphin Tribe, feeling privileged to have met them. Sergio and Paulo, both excellent photographers, took dozens of photographs. These lovely, knowledgeable people lived isolated and untouched by the outside world with the exception of Ana who had been living with them briefly and the Peruvian police who kept everyone else away. At least they were being protected now.

On our way back, we stopped at the first Indian village we had visited and purchased some bananas from our new friends. Our pink dolphin guides reappeared, circled our canoe and disappeared again, just as a pair of slow-moving Amazonian manatees surfaced for air and followed our canoe until we reached the main Putumayo River. These gentle, aquatic, herbivore mammals weigh up to 1000 pounds and are found exclusively in the freshwater of the Amazon region. They say if you want to find the rare Amazonian manatee, you must first make peace with the pink river dolphin because the dolphin is considered the manatee's guardian. I felt honored to have encountered both. Many indigenous Amazonian tribes revere dolphins to be sacred animals and consider it very bad luck to kill a dolphin and even worse—to eat one. It is said that their shaman learn their medicinal techniques from the dolphins. The Amazonian pink river dolphins are also known to be shapeshifters that will sometimes whisk young children away to a magical underwater city called Encante, where they will live the rest of their lives, never to return to land again. In that moment I wanted to be taken by the dolphins to live in Encante too.

Reluctantly, we left the mythical realm of the Dolphin Tribe and arrived at the Peruvian police border outpost. It consisted of two shacks on the top of a hill overlooking the Putumayo River. The police officer lived in one building with his wife and two young children. He told us to stay in the other building while he took our passports and checked us out. We hung up our hammocks and waited for four days.

*** 

On the third evening, the Peruvian policeman offered to take Isabela out in a canoe to see the wildlife. She was excited to go. Pedro wasn't interested in going. He had grown distant since we almost lost him in the river. The Peruvian policeman took Isabela out alone at night in his canoe. Isabela was very quiet when she returned and finally told us that he had raped her in the canoe.

I naively asked, "Why didn't you scream or fight him off?"

She told me that she had no choice. After he had paddled the canoe some distance away from where we were staying, he had shone his flashlight across the water so she could see the red eyes of the dozens of caiman surrounding them. He threatened to throw her out of the canoe for the caiman to eat if she didn't oblige his desire. If she had struggled, the canoe would have tipped over. I was shocked. We had trusted this policeman. He was the only law here and he still had our passports. There was nothing any of us could do. I felt terrified and helpless.

Paulo learned from the policeman's wife that a small monthly seaplane to Iquitos, Peru, was going to arrive the next day. He decided to go with it, as did Isabela. She was ready to return to France. Pedro and Christian decided to fly away with them to Iquitos too. Christian claimed he was leaving us, because being a French chef, he was frustrated that we didn't have enough interesting food left for him to cook. It is true he had been traveling with black pepper he brought from France and we were living on mostly green bananas, maize, and any fish that we caught. Still, it seemed a pretty lame excuse to me.

I was undecided. I was still loving our canoe adventure and Sergio and I had fallen in love with each other. I would have been perfectly happy, if it were not for the treacherous policeman and the hungry mosquitoes that had started biting since the rains began. It had become necessary for me to wear a long-sleeve shirt, straw hat, pants, socks, and shoes all day to protect myself from them. The mosquitoes still attacked my hands and neck. At least, I had rid myself of most of the yellow spiders that were buried in my skin. Something deep inside my adventurous soul refused to let me leave. The river still called to me and pulled me to continue on. I was determined to get to Leticia by water.

That night, Christian used the very last of our spaghetti, onion, and his spices to make a tasty meal of pasta and curried fish. This was the last meal we all shared together.

*** 

The day of their flight, the entire Dolphin Tribe arrived in their dugout canoes with Ana to see the plane off. Before the seaplane landed on the river, the tribe visited with us. They were fascinated with my tent and notebook. One woman carrying a woolly monkey was captivated by my comb so I let her use it. I only had one comb with me, otherwise I would have given it to her. She used it to comb her hair and then gave it back to me.

When the amphibious plane took off from the river with Paulo, Christian, Isabella, and Pedro, the tribe's children ran joyfully along the shore behind it with outstretched arms imitating flying birds. I wondered how long this untouched, remote tribe would survive before they forgot their ancient ways and flew blindly into the society of the modern world.

*Indigenous boy fishing in the river.*

# Chapter 11

# Down to Four—Jungle Madness

## _Ana_

_Looking through_

_the stained eyes_

_of paranoid illusion,_

_she coiled_

_struck_

_then hid in the tall grass,_

_waiting for_

_impenetrable darkness_

_to cover_

_her flight._

Ana told us she was ready to leave the Dolphin Tribe and asked if she could join our canoe trip. Sergio, Jose, and I readily agreed. She was familiar with river life and we could manage better with another person along to paddle. Ana told us that if we traveled for just another ten days, we could reach El Estrecho, Peru, where there should be big boats traveling to Leticia on the Amazon.

Previously, on this journey along the river, I asked the people we met how far it was to the next farm or town. I was never given an answer in miles which irritated me. I wanted to know the mileage. Instead, I was told how many days it took to get there by canoe. Later, when I finally saw a map of the meandering Putumayo River, I understood why. This river, especially in the dry season, was so winding that a town only a few miles away as the crow flies, could take days to get to by canoe.

\*\*\*

We set out in Chiclet early the following morning. By the end of the day we reached the village of Puerto Alegria, Colombia. It was beginning to dawn on us that it was going to be very difficult for just the four of us to safely manage our huge canoe on the ever-widening Putumayo River.

We found a place to set up an overnight camp in an open area where there were several local men drinking beer. They were friendly enough, so we felt safe camping there, especially because some of the men were the local police. They asked to see our passports, looked at them briefly, then watched us put our documents into my tent. They returned to their beverages and proceeded to get quite drunk.

One of the men, Guillermo, hospitably invited us to come eat supper at his house. We cleaned ourselves up with a bath in the river and set off on the jungle trail he had told us to follow. As dark began to descend, the dusk mosquitoes attacked us relentlessly. After a long walk we finally arrived at his house, but to our disappointment it was a completely unfinished frame of a house and no one was there. We turned around and headed back to our campsite only to run into Guillermo on his way home. We returned with him to his half-finished house, where he cooked us an excellent meal on an open fire. After eating, we managed to navigate our way back to our campsite in the dark, only to discover that our passports, money, travelers checks, my drawing pens and journal had all been stolen. We immediately reported our loss to the local police and they did nothing.

\*\*\*

The next day, Ana came down with a high fever, a grim-looking infection on her hand, and big inflamed red spots all over her body. Jose also developed a high fever. The multitude of ever-increasing mosquitoes became more and more aggressive. They were horrible. I was glad I had started taking malaria pills before we left Puerto Asis.

The police continued to do nothing about our stolen items, so I decided our best move to help motivate them was to set up camp in the shack on the edge of town that was both their police station and the home of the police chief who was away on a trip downriver. We moved in, and while the others hung up their laundry and hammocks, I pitched my tent outside in front.

\*\*\*

Three days later, the surly police, apparently with the help of two local children, finally found our passports, travelers checks, and my journal on a jungle trail. None of our stolen cash was returned. I was still missing $50 and Sergio lost the equivalent in Brazilian cruzeiros. It was a fishy story. I think the real reason they returned our passports was because they wanted us to move out of the police station.

In fact, the police told us we had to leave immediately. I suspected that their police chief was expected home soon and they knew he was not going to appreciate us living in his house/police station. Additionally, they were concerned that whatever was making Ana and Jose sick was contagious. This theory had inadvertently been spread by me, because I had gone around telling everyone that we needed help because Ana had sarampo which means measles. I had no idea that measles could be fatal, especially in an isolated jungle village with no doctors or medicine.

It was an impossible situation with two sick people, no money, and no food. Travelers checks were useless in the jungle. No one would take them, which is probably why the police had returned them to us. Puerto Alegria had no motorboat and no radio—no form of communication with the outside world.

I didn't know what we should do. We desperately wanted to leave, but could not. Ana and Jose were now both much too sick to travel. They were bedridden and we had no idea what they were actually suffering from. Sergio and I did all we could to take care of them under these horrific conditions. The rainy season had begun in full force, bringing a torrential downpour every afternoon. The showers were cool and refreshing, but the standing pools of water created by the rain helped the breeding mosquitoes to multiply and become more intolerable.

The only food we could find were avocados from a big tree growing beside the police station. I love avocados, but these avocados were as hard as rocks and much too green to even attempt to eat.

Sergio and I helped our new friend Guillermo to build the roof for his house in exchange for food for all of us. If not for Guillermo's generosity we would have gone hungry. After his palm frond roof was finished, we cut bamboo canes and dragged them back to his property to build a fence. It was exhausting work in the hot jungle. I returned home each day ready to drop.

Ana and Jose did not improve. We had done everything we could think of to help them get well. The police kept pressuring us to leave, but there was no way Sergio and I could manage our big canoe without assistance.

One evening Ana cried out to me in a weak voice, "I am going to die in this hell of Puerto Alegria."

I believed her. I was worried out of my mind. Jose stayed in bed all day long and said nothing. Their high fevers raged on. We could wait no longer. We had to find a way to leave before Ana and Jose died in this desolate place.

Sergio and I asked everyone we could find for someone to help us move our canoe downstream. We finally found two local men who, for 200 pesos, agreed to guide us in our canoe to a place where there was a motor with gasoline. We needed to get Ana and Jose to a place where they could get medical attention very soon.

The evening before we left, Guillermo helped us build a palm leaf shade cover for our canoe to protect our two invalids from the sun and rain while we traveled. I made a meager supper with the last of our food. Ana refused to eat anything. I continued to worry that she might never recover. A foreboding heavy rain drummed hard on my tent all night.

\*\*\*

In the morning a cherry bright sun greeted us, but only one of the guides showed up and he wanted more money. This was distressing as we had already been robbed in this inhospitable place and had very little cash left. With only one man to help us, Sergio and I were going to have to do all of the paddling, all day long.

We couldn't wait any longer and were eventually forced to leave with just one guide. As he took over the stern of our canoe, he put some coca leaves into his mouth. Coca leaves are the main ingredient of the drug cocaine. Chewing coca leaves to suppress hunger, thirst, pain, and fatigue is a deeply rooted tradition in this part of the world going back thousands of years.

Sergio and I took our positions at the front of the canoe while Jose and Ana slept in the middle. We paddled and paddled and paddled. With such a large canoe, it was extremely difficult for so few people to maneuver it. Previously we had rotated the work of paddling the canoe every hour or so whenever anyone got tired. Now Sergio and I had to do all of the work ceaselessly. I wished that our guide would share some of his coca leaves, but he didn't offer.

After a long five hours, our guide sighted the house that owned the motor on the Colombian side of the river. Yes, there was a motor, but of course, it had no gasoline and none was going to be arriving until later in the rainy season when big boats could bring supplies upriver.

The people who owned the motor told us that there was a Peruvian outpost about an hour downstream with medicine. Our guide refused to go any further. He said he had just agreed to take us to a motor, which he had done. His job was over.

I looked over at Jose and Ana as they weakly watched us from the canoe. Neither of them was strong enough to steer or paddle. Our big canoe needed a minimum of three people to navigate it. In desperation I reached out and grabbed the pouch where I had seen our guide put his money. I refused to return it to him unless he continued with us. After a long, loud argument he finally agreed to go as far as the Peruvian outpost.

When we eventually arrived, I was completely drained and my hands were covered in raw blisters from padding nonstop all day. Everyone at this Peruvian outpost was drunk, celebrating the arrival of their first trading boat of the rainy season. Sergio and our guide joined the celebration while I sought out a medic for our invalids.

I was relieved to discover that Ana seemed somewhat revived after resting in the canoe all day. Disappointingly though, she adamantly refused to take the medicine the medic offered her, and began to complain angrily about our situation. Jose, on the other hand, was grateful to us for getting him there and readily took the medicine he was given.

Luckily, the trading boat was leaving the next day for El Encanto, Colombia. We had no choice. We simply could not continue on in our canoe. With a tear in my eye, we sold our beautiful dugout, Chiclet for next to nothing. We had lived in that old dugout canoe for almost a month and a half. She had taken us so far and through so many adventures I found it hard to say farewell.

\*\*\*

The next day we all went downriver in the trading boat. The Peruvian people on this little barge were very friendly and helpful—completely different from the people we had encountered in Puerto Alegria, with the exception of Guillermo. Our boat stopped frequently to trade sugar and coffee with the locals we passed, in exchange for a variety of animal skins and fledgling green Amazon parrots fated for the pet trade. Having seen these beautiful, intelligent birds flying at liberty together in family groups overhead, I found myself deeply saddened when I saw them caged, destined to be sent far away from their true rainforest home.

After a few days our boat arrived in El Encanto. The local police here generously gave us a house to stay in with screened windows, running water, and a flush toilet! Such luxuries! It was especially wonderful to have screened windows as mosquitoes were everywhere outside.

Ana had by now pretty much recovered from her red spot ailment which turned out to be, not measles or any contagious disease, but an allergic reaction to mosquito bites. I think she must have also been suffering from jungle madness. The day after we arrived in El Encanto she suddenly declared that she was invisible and now that she was well, she wanted nothing more to do with any of us. She insisted she was going to disappear. She proclaimed that she hated the people of Colombia and Peru as well as the gracious Dolphin Tribe who had so generously hosted her for a month. She also hated Sergio, Jose, and me.

Jose's fever had finally broken and his infected hand was healing. He was feeling much better. He had shown all the symptoms of malaria: shaking chills, high fever, profuse sweating, and a headache with nausea. As he had not been taking anti-malaria pills it is highly likely that he had been suffering a bad malarial episode. Unlike Ana, his illness had made him humble and appreciative.

Sergio and I had been entirely responsible for feeding, caring for, and transporting Jose and Ana when they were deathly ill. We youthfully declared to each other that we would never ever have any children. It was too much work. These challenging times of hardship had brought us closer together and strengthened our new burgeoning love.

On our first night in the house, Jose cooked what he called his traditional famous Spanish omelet. It was delicious and filling. I had never had an omelet with potatoes in it before. That evening, as Sergio washed up our dirty dishes, there was an epic thunderstorm. A giant bolt of lightning hit the frame of the open window where he was working. The nearness of the electricity left his hands shaking uncontrollably for some time. He felt lucky to be alive and we all made jokes about how dangerous it was to wash dishes.

*\*\*\**

We had to wait a few more days until we could catch another boat to take us downriver, so Sergio and I decided to do some exploring in the jungle around El Encanto. We hiked into the wilds until we found a narrow footpath that was almost completely hidden by lush tropical greenery. We had not gone far on this trail when we discovered a large hidden building with a round palm covered roof. I peeked inside and saw men stirring big piles of leaves on the floor. I was fascinated and wanted to go inside and ask them what they were doing.

Sergio grabbed my arm and whispered, "No, we must go now. Be quiet!"

Not having a clue as to what I was seeing, I didn't want to listen to him, but there was something in his urgent insistence that made me follow him silently away. Later he explained that they were rendering harvested coca leaves to make illegal cocaine. We had been lucky not to be seen or our lives might have been in danger. We promptly ended our little jungle exploration and returned to town.

I wondered if the friendly local police who had given us a house to stay in, were in cahoots with these nearby cocaine makers. This was very early in the lucrative days of Colombia's illegal production and exportation of cocaine. The Medellin and Cali Cartels were just getting started back in 1976. The Putumayo area later became extremely important in the cocaine trade, producing nearly 70% of the world's coca leaf. If we had traveled on this river just a few years later, the little farms growing corn and rice that we had passed earlier upstream would have changed their crop to the much more profitable coca plant. Our canoe trip would have been dangerously impossible.

That night, for the first time, I had a dream in Spanish. They say if you dream in a new language then you are thinking in it and really making progress with learning it. I was pleased with myself, however, the next morning I didn't feel well enough to even get out of bed. My head was spinning in pain. I felt exhausted. Ana made me some rice with caramel which was delicious, but I was still feeling hurt after what she had said to me earlier. It seemed that she had not made this food for me out of friendship, but more out of a sense of obligation, because I had cared for her when she was sick. Sergio didn't believe that I was really sick. He thought that it was all in my head. I think the truth was that he didn't want to be responsible for another sick person again.

I came down with a terrible fever and pain all over my body. I couldn't eat anything. Finally, my friends got a medic from the town to come to see me. He took my temperature, listened to my heart, took my blood pressure, and then strangely, without saying a single word, left. I wondered if I would ever see him again.

Before too long, the medic returned with antibiotics and vitamins for me. He diagnosed me as suffering from malnutrition and a serious bladder infection. Feeling guilty for not believing that I was truly ill, Sergio tried to make amends by cooking me a lovely meal. I wanted to show my appreciation, but I was too sick to eat a single bite.

*** 

The next day the barge we had been waiting for arrived. It was going to be in El Encanto for just one night and was departing for Leticia, Colombia, early the next morning. I was still too ill to visit the boat, but Sergio talked with the captain late into the night and arranged free passage for both of us. After being robbed in Puerto Alegria we didn't have much cash left at all. Sergio managed to work out a deal with the captain where we would just have to pay for our food on the boat. Early the next morning, before it was light, the four of us took a small dugout taxi canoe, out to the barge, arriving just in time to get on board before it left for Leticia.

*Peruvian outpost on the Putumayo River.*

# Chapter 12

# Rio Amazonas in Brazil

*The sky breaks open*
*with golden light*
*illuminating my Amazon*
*stretching like an ocean*
*water shelter to an unknown life*
*Freedom, Freedom*
*free my heart*
*Let it fly!*

The captain of our Colombian barge was a jovial fellow who traveled with his large wife and their two young children. Our other shipmates included Jose, Ana, a woman with two children, several men, and one of the friendly policemen who had given us the house to stay in El Encanto. This policeman had patiently waited a month and a half for the rainy season to return, so he could catch this barge. All of us were happy to be back on the river.

There were also two adorable baby coatimundis living with us on the barge. They played with each other, racing all over the boat, entertaining us with their engaging, energetic antics. Coatimundis are tropical cousins of the raccoon, with a long flexible snout and striped tail they carry high above their bodies. Regrettably, these cute juveniles had been stolen from their mother who in all likelihood was killed during their abduction, so her babies could be sold downriver as pets.

I spent much of my time writing in my journal which surprisingly attracted a great deal of attention because I wrote with my left hand. The crew and other passengers on our barge were fascinated because they had never seen anyone write with their left hand before. As our boat continued toward Brazil, the interminable heat became so unbearable that I could not continue writing. My perspiration dripped so profusely, that it actually blurred my pen's ink on the pages, turning my words into illegible pools of blue tears.

Sergio and I didn't have a hammock, so at night we were forced to sleep on the cold, hard steel floor of the barge. Our first fight was over which one of us got the sack of dry beans for a pillow. Barely able to sleep in these spartan conditions, we fantasized about how wonderful it was going to be when we got to Manaus, Brazil, where we dreamed of staying in an expensive hotel with a soft bed and a real bathroom with a hot shower.

The medicine I had been given by the medic in El Encanto was working, so I was feeling better, but I still had tiny yellow spiders embedded in my skin and my head was itchy. I could not understand why my head was continuously itchy until Sergio told me he saw lice in my hair. I was both horrified and embarrassed. I didn't want anyone on the barge to know I had lice. I wondered where I might have picked up these parasites until I remembered sharing my comb with the Dolphin Tribe woman. Did I get lice from her or the woolly monkey she had in her arms? I never knew for sure. The feeling of lice crawling all over my head and not having any way to get rid of them, until we reached our destination in Leticia was an incessant nightmare that I would not wish on anyone.

The only entertainment we had on this slow-moving barge was BINGO which was played every night. Sergio and I became bored with doing nothing all day, so to alleviate our boredom we offered to wash dishes, peel potatoes, and help with the daily meals of rice and fish. The good-natured captain proclaimed that for our kitchen work he would give us not only free passage, but also free food. He was a good man.

The lush, tangled shoreline we passed grew increasingly dense as we left Colombia and entered into the Brazilian part of the river. Being in a new country excited me and my mood improved even more when a pod of pink river dolphins surprised us by popping up to lead our way from the mouth of the Putumayo into the largest river in the world—the Amazon. Compared to the Putumayo River, this river was like an ocean. It was several miles wide! I had finally reached the destination I had dreamed about for years: the Amazon River.

*Alycin in the Amazon Rainforest.*

Our first night on the Amazon we ate a freshly killed Paca that had been caught when we stopped briefly on shore. Pacas are cute, spotted, herbivore rodents that are highly prized as bushmeat by the people who live along the river. I hated to see the poor creature killed, but I was also relieved to have a break from eating fish for every meal, every single day. My vegetarian days were over.

***

After nine long exceptionally uncomfortable nights we finally arrived in Leticia, Colombia. When our boat docked, Ana and Jose left us, each heading in a different direction. As soon as I got off the barge, the first thing I did was to race to a pharmacy and purchase the only thing they had that killed lice—a bottle of pure DDT. It had been banned in North America but was still readily available in this jungle town. We checked into Hotel Leticia, a clean place, with comfortable beds and no mosquitoes. Weighing the dangers of potential cancer over ridding myself of the nasty parasites that were driving me crazy, I risked my life and showered, pouring the DDT all over my head and body. It worked surprisingly well. Both the lice and yellow skin spiders were gone with one treatment. DDT was great stuff. Lord knows what it did to my liver.

Most of our cash had been stolen in Puerto Alegria, but we still had some American Express travelers checks which had been impossible to use in the jungle. We were finally able to cash them here at the bank and after getting our money, Sergio and I considered what we should do next. We were both exhausted after living in a canoe or boat in these South American waters for over two months. Completely fed up with the hardships of river travel the next day, in a moment of madness we spent most of our money on plane tickets to Manaus, Brazil. I know it sounds foolish, but at the time I felt guilty for flying and not traveling by river the seven hundred miles from Leticia to Manaus.

***

When we arrived in Manaus, I phoned home to let my worried parents know I was still alive. As it was now mid-March, we had missed Brazilian Carnival but I didn't mind. I loved the old city of Manaus. It was first founded in 1669 as a European settlement called Fort of Sao Jose do Rio Negro, and in 1832 it was elevated to a town, with a new name of Manaus derived from the local indigenous Manáos people. This remarkable, isolated city is situated in the heart of the Amazon rainforest, just north of where the Black River meets the Amazon River.

On our first day we enjoyed taking in the sights of the city as we walked along its beautiful black and white mosaic sidewalks. In the 19th century, Manaus had been the home of Brazil's powerful rubber barons. With their incredible wealth, they had turned this remote Amazonian metropolis into a place with expensive, enchanting architecture. The most spectacular building by far is Teatro Amazonas, the Manaus Opera house. It is a fantastic theatre with one hundred and ninety-eight crystal chandeliers, some of which were made from imported Venetian Murano glass.

That evening we went to see an opera singer perform at Teatro Amazonas. The theatre inside was magnificent, with huge chandeliers, marble columns, red velvet seats, and rows of private box seats surrounding the stage. The incredible hand-painted theatre backdrop *The Meeting of the Waters* created in Paris by Crispim do Amaral was mesmerizing.

While we were out enjoying the city, someone broke into our hotel room and stole Sergio's Pentax camera, sunglasses, and my blue jeans. The police did not arrive until the next day. Sergio tried to get the hotel to replace his camera, but the maid said there had never been a camera in our room. I suspected she was in cahoots with the thief. The saddest thing about losing his camera was that all of the film Sergio and Paulo had used to take the irreplaceable photos of the primitive Dolphin Tribe were still in the camera.

\*\*\*

After five days, the police still had done nothing about Sergio's stolen camera. When the owner of the hotel said that the maid had seen me enter the room with the key and take the camera, I became absolutely furious and could stand it no longer. I shouted loudly: "SENOR! YOU ARE LYING!" and promptly pulled out my Canadian passport and told the Brazilian police officer to call my embassy. Slightly intimidated, the officer finally agreed that he was responsible for my protection and the hotel was responsible for our belongings and there had certainly been a robbery. He then told the manager of the hotel to buy Sergio a new cheap camera.

Sergio exploded with an alarming anger I had never seen before. He strongly demanded that the hotel buy him the same Pentax camera that had been stolen. He used Portuguese words I didn't understand, but their meaning was clear. He went too far for a Brazilian. The policeman stood up, and with quivering nostrils told Sergio he was asking for a beating. This was a frightening move, because at that time torture and police brutality were not at all uncommon under the Brazilian military dictatorship. Unnerved, Sergio said not another word. The policeman then told the hotel manager to buy Sergio a new camera or go to court to settle it. The hotel manager agreed to give Sergio money to buy a new Pentax camera.

After Sergio purchased a new camera, we were both ready to leave the corruption of city life and head back into the wilds of the Amazon rainforest. I felt there was an undertone of a survivalist mentality among many people in Manaus. Perhaps this was because the city was inhabited by numerous people who, like us, had spent almost all of their money to get there and then found themselves trapped in this jungle city with no money or way to leave.

The first road to Manaus was not inaugurated until later 1976 and this new dirt track through the jungle was impassable during the rainy season. The only way for us to get out of Manaus was by plane or boat. The mouth of the Amazon River was nine hundred miles away, east of us on the Atlantic Ocean. It made the most sense for us to head south. As there were no buses or trains, we looked for a boat and found one that would take us toward Bolivia. Before leaving we bought a big comfortable two-person Brazilian hammock. I did not want to spend another night on the hard, cold floor of a barge again.

***

The following day we departed on a barge that was heading to Puerto Velho, Brazil. We crossed the black waters of the Black River to reach the Amazon River as we left Manaus. The Black River really does have black-tea-colored water, and as we crossed into the Amazon River, I could see a distinct line of its dark water against the brown waters of the Amazon.

That night Sergio and I slept in our new double hammock. It was so big that once we were in it, we thought we could not be seen. Apparently, we could be both seen and heard because as our passions progressed in our hanging bed, the ship's captain quite suddenly turned off all the lights on the boat. We laughed and carried on.

***

The next morning after a comfortable sleep, we found ourselves on the Madeira River. It was good to be out of the city, surrounded by the rainforest again. We crossed the state of

Amazonas to Puerto Velho in the state of Rondonia, Brazil, where we expected our next barge to be waiting for us, but our connecting boat was not there. This was a serious problem due to the visa limitations on Sergio's Brazilian passport. He was required to exit Brazil by or before the following Saturday, or he was not going to be allowed to leave the country. The barge we needed was not expected to arrive until his deadline of Saturday, and there was no guarantee that it would arrive then. If Sergio was not permitted to leave Brazil with me, I didn't know if I should continue on alone to Bolivia or stay with him in Brazil. This possibility made me consider more deeply where our relationship was headed. I wasn't really sure how I felt or what I should do.

# Chapter 13
# Nazi in A Separate Reality

"The aim is to balance the terror of being alive with
the wonder of being alive."—Carlos Castaneda.

The barge we needed arrived just in time to meet Sergio's strict Brazilian visa exit requirements, so I was not compelled to make a decision as to whether I would stay with Sergio or leave him behind and travel to Bolivia alone.

Our new boat left Puerto Velho, Brazil, and headed upriver toward Bolivia. We were on this small barge long enough to become acquainted with all of the other passengers. There was a woman traveling with three young children who I got to know fairly well. The mother of these children was quite strange and appeared to be living in a world of her own most of the time. I surmised that she had been living in the jungle much too long. She sat all day just staring into space while her children played completely unsupervised and running all over the barge. I was concerned that one of the little ones might fall off the boat into the river, so I tried to entertain them by playing games with them.

The eldest girl who was about eight years old didn't understand when I needed a break. She pestered me incessantly, by continually poking at me with her fingers, not unlike the swarms of mosquitoes that constantly irritated me until I could stand it no longer. There was no place to escape the insects or her insistent poking and finally I spun around and shouted much too loudly: "Para! Stop it!"

She backed away crying and I felt horrible. Poor child, she desperately needed attention and I had hurt her feelings. I tried to apologize, but it was too late. No doubt she had been rejected and hit in the past and I had broken the fragile trust she had with me.

The girl's mother later explained that she was on this boat with her children because she was leaving her abusive husband and had no money. I didn't have much money myself, but I also didn't have three children dependent on me. I gave her what I could and she gave me an enchanting necklace made of hand-carved animals decorated with black tipped scarlet seeds. She told me that this necklace had been made by Amazon Indians and possessed magical powers. I later learned that the colorful seeds in my unique necklace were actually extremely poisonous Jequirity beans. Luckily, I didn't chew on them!

Sergio developed a terrible eye infection that the locals said was caused by an insect they called a firefly. His right eye swelled up beyond recognition. It became an angry red with yellow pus oozing profusely out of it. He looked like some kind of horrible monster. I felt sorry for him and I know it was entirely unfair of me, but my physical attraction to him diminished completely. I could hardly bear to look at him, let alone let him kiss me. There was so much disease in the Amazon Basin we never knew what we would pick up next.

Our barge stopped at every small settlement we passed along the river to deliver goods and trade. One evening in the middle of nowhere, while we were stopped at a nameless place in the jungle, Sergio and I went into a house where one could buy drinks. By this time his infected eye was pretty much healed so he looked human again.

There was an odd old man with gray hair and white skin in this little bar. He seemed completely out of place, but I wasn't initially entirely sure why. He was captivated by my blonde hair and blue eyes and offered to buy drinks for Sergio and I. He proceeded to get exceedingly drunk and began to talk lovingly about Germany from where he had originated. When his eyes began to sparkle and he emphasized his comments with a smile for me and the Hitler salute, I became frightened. We quickly left and returned to our barge. We never saw or heard from him again.

In retrospect, I have no doubt that he was a Nazi hiding in the jungle. After World War II, many Nazis fled to several countries in South America along the so-called ratline escape routes to find sanctuary. Had we met the sadistic Butcher of Lyon, Klaus Barbie? It was very possible, because Barbie was in fact captured in Bolivia seven years later. When I described the man we had met to my father, who had been General Montgomery's driver in France during the war, he suggested with alarm that we had quite likely met Barbie. I sometimes wonder if I should have reported seeing him, but I didn't even know the name of the place where we had met him. At the time, all I could think about was getting far away from this old lunatic Nazi who had taken a fancy to me.

We continued up the Madera River into the Mamore River, eventually arriving at the town of Trinidad, Bolivia. After three months in the Amazon rainforest, Sergio and I were both more than ready to leave our barge and the jungle behind. I sent my parents a letter from Trinidad which initially confused them. They, like many, had never heard of Trinidad, Bolivia, and wondered how I had managed to get to a Caribbean island by boat from Manaus, Brazil!

From Trinidad we made our way overland up to the highest capital city in the world: La Paz, Bolivia. After reaching the city's high elevation, I came down with altitude sickness and a cold which made me feel quite miserable for a few days, but I loved Bolivia. The people were calm, hardworking, and strong. We stayed in a cheap hotel in La Paz where we were surprised to run into our old canoe buddy, Christian! He was broke and planning to hitchhike through Bolivia to Argentina. He told us he was engaged to a beautiful Peruvian woman and madly in love. She was unfortunately still in Peru.

Christian had some cactus with him called San Pedro that he said had been given to him by a Q'ero Incan shaman on the Andean slopes of Peru. The shaman had advised him that some of the most important messages he would ever encounter during his lifetime would be received when he took this enchanted cactus. I was familiar with San Pedro's cactus cousin, the hallucinogen peyote, but I had never heard of San Pedro before. Christian insisted we all eat some together that night, so we did.

After about two hours it started to affect me. Wow! The drugs that anthropologist Carlos Castanada took on his magical journey, described in his book, *A Separate Reality* were tame compared to this powerful San Pedro. I began to tune into messages from my female ancestors. Every traumatic moment that my grandmothers, great-grandmothers, and great-great-grandmothers had experienced was revealed to me. Prior to this I had never really thought much about them. My maternal grandmother had died before I was born and I was three when my paternal grandmother had passed away. I had never met any of my great-grandmothers. Suddenly, with the help of San Pedro, I completely understood and felt all of the pain and challenges that these strong women had suffered during their lifetimes. I wept uncontrollably for hours.

When I stopped crying, San Pedro appeared to me as an ancient shaman and told me the true story of creation. He explained in a vision that the Sun Mother had created the universe with her warm yellow power. She made the plants and animals, including humans and sent them all to the earth in a giant canoe. This special canoe was actually a giant Anaconda snake that swam in the river of life while the newly created beings rode inside. Eventually the living snake-canoe became weary from this long tiring journey of life, stopped at a high waterfall and opened its mouth to yawn. As the snake-canoe yawned, all of the people and animals inside ran out to travel to different parts of the river to live. Each person had been given one possession to help them live on earth. Some had a bow and arrow, others had a fishing pole, some had blowguns, and some had drums. San Pedro went on to explain that some people had come to earth already knowing what fish, plants, and wild fruits were safe to eat. The Sun Mother gave women a special knowledge of how to use specific plants to practice birth control, because if they had more than two or three children, she would not send game for them to hunt.

Finally, my San Pedro guide explained that the Sun Mother had taught the first people how to use hallucinogenic plants in order to communicate with the many other supernatural beings in the universe. He continued to tell me that the Sun Mother had created these special mind-expanding plants to protect the earth, so that people like me could hallucinate and contact spirits from both the past and the future. It all made perfect sense at the time.

Sixteen hours later, I remembered everything that I had experienced and learned. I was left with an enormous new appreciation for all of my grandmothers. The magical San Pedro cactus had connected me with the deeply encoded DNA genetic memories of my indestructible female ancestors. A new story of creation had been revealed, which was conceivably just as plausible as the story in the Bible. It was a most remarkable mystical trip that permanently affected my perceptions of life thereafter.

*Alycin listening to San Pedro.*

\*\*\*

Following this mystical experience, I was ready to continue with my South American travels. Sergio and I thanked Christian for the remarkable San Pedro encounter and bade him goodbye. We traveled 500 km by bus from La Paz to Potosí, Bolivia, where the charming locals still wore colorful, handwoven ponchos. Potosí, the highest city in Bolivia was once one of the richest cities in the world when it was a colonial silver mining town that was founded in 1546. Throughout the next 200 years, more than 40,000 tons of silver were shipped to Spain. The silver was taken by llama to the Pacific coast, shipped north to Panama, carried by mule train across Panama, and then shipped to Spain, making the Spanish Empire one of the wealthiest, most powerful nations in the world. Yet for all the wealth the mine had created, most of the people in Potosí were living in poverty. They still work the mine, but most of the silver is long gone and the only mineral left to mine is tin, which is much less valuable.

It snowed our last night in Potosí. This was the first time Sergio had ever seen snow. I purchased a beautiful wool Potosí poncho to keep warm before we took a chilly all-night bus ride under a full moon, across the dusty Bolivian high desert. We arrived at the border of Bolivia and Argentina at dawn. I was completely unaware that Argentina was in the middle of a treacherous civil unrest that resulted in 30,000 people disappearing after being brutally tortured and subsequently murdered by the military.

# Chapter 14
# *Don't Cry for Me, Argentina*

*Like a moth to a flame*

*I return to you again, and again, and again and again*

*The closer I get*

*The further your light*

*I never learn to avoid your pain*

*Like a moth to a flame*

*I return my love again, and again, and again*

After securing an exit visa stamp from the Bolivian police, we walked across a bridge to La Quiaca, Argentina, where the road abruptly changed from dirt to asphalt. Without asking me a single question, the Argentine immigration officer stamped my passport with a three-month tourist visa. I was excited and eager to explore this new country.

With only $40 left, I decided the best way to conserve money was to hitchhike to our next destination, Buenos Aires. I was nervous about hitchhiking across the mountainous, dry desert because a Bolivian man had warned us it was not safe. But because that was the same message we'd received from everyone who had never hitchhiked, we didn't let it stop us. Had he told us that revolutionary guerrillas were hiding in the northern mountains near the border we had just crossed, we might have listened. Fortunately, we didn't run into them!

Instead, we met some friendly truck drivers who generously offered us a ride 300 km south to Jujui, Argentina, where they were required to stop to wait for cargo. As it was getting dark and they still didn't have the cargo they were waiting for, Sergio and I found a cheap hotel with a hot shower, washed off the dirt of the road and got a good night's sleep.

***

Early the next morning, our truck drivers had already left, so we set out for the main road on our own to start hitchhiking. I noticed that several of the buildings we walked past had VOTE PERON spray-painted on the walls as graffiti. We did not know that on March 24, 1976, a week before our arrival, there had been a right-wing coup d'état that had overthrown the president of Argentina, Isabel Perón, and placed her under arrest. Isabel, the third wife of the late President Juan Perón, had taken over as president of Argentina when her husband had been on his deathbed in 1974. She was the first female head of government in the Western Hemisphere. After her arrest a brutal military junta was installed to replace her. It was an exceptionally dangerous time to be in Argentina.

The police at the edge of town checked our passports and sent us walking out into the desert where the road suddenly changed again, this time from asphalt to dirt. We played a game of chess for five hours as we sat in the sun by the dusty road waiting for a ride that never came.

Eventually we gave up, returned to town and purchased train tickets to Buenos Aires. No doubt, it was fortuitous that we were forced to take the train or who knows what might have happened to us hitchhiking in this isolated mountainous semi-desert part of northern Argentina.

\*\*\*

When we arrived in Buenos Aires, I sent my parents a telegram asking them to send me $500 from my bank account to the Banco De La Nation, Argentina. They wired me back immediately to let me know that the money had been telexed to the bank. I waited as my remaining meager funds dwindled, checking daily at the bank for my money. Sergio, who was also running out of money, became impatient. He decided to leave for his home in Santos, Brazil, with an invitation for me to come visit him there when my money arrived. I told Sergio I was fine, still confident that my money would arrive imminently. I had started this trip solo and missed having time to think, write, and contemplate the thoughts one can only have unaccompanied. Nevertheless, I was not sure how I felt about Sergio deciding to leave me, almost penniless and alone in Buenos Aires.

As I waited for my money to arrive, I explored the beautiful old capital. Even though the county was in political turmoil, the people seemed perfectly normal shopping and carrying on as one does anywhere. One day while window shopping in the walkable shopping district on Calle Florida, close to the famous Plaza de Mayo, I heard a sudden loud bang and crackle. In an instant, every casual shopper around me on the street dropped flat to the ground and didn't move. *What happened? Were they shot?* I remained standing, stunned—a solitary statue, not comprehending what was happening. Silently, the crowd slowly got up as they realized that it had not been gunfire, but rather an electric transformer that had exploded nearby. In a few minutes the street returned to normal as if nothing had happened. The normalness I had witnessed previously was just a brave facade. Everyone was on edge, ready to drop or hide at a moment's notice.

As my funds continued to diminish, I appreciated how inexpensive everything was in Buenos Aires. The hotel I stayed in cost only fifty cents a night and a decent meal in a restaurant was just twenty-five cents. Good wine was cheaper than Pepsi Cola. One day I went into a big restaurant and was happily surprised to see my former canoe buddies Janice and Suzanne. I joined them for a meal and we caught up with our travel stories.

They had made it to Rio de Janeiro, Brazil, in time to celebrate carnival, which takes place every year during the five days that lead up to Ash Wednesday and the start of Lent. Both had enjoyed a fabulous time dancing night and day to live Samba music with costumed Brazilians on parade in the streets of Rio. On their way to Argentina they had visited Paulo in Santos. Now they were heading to Chile. Like me, they were traveling frugally, so when the man sitting next to us left his table, Suzanne reached over and grabbed one of his untouched fresh buns that she assumed had been paid for and abandoned. We didn't notice that he had tipped his chair against the table, which in a Buenos Aires restaurant means the diner will be returning. When Janice noticed him coming back to his table from the bathroom, she quickly stuffed the bun up her shirt and we left in a hurry, embarrassed and giggling. The next day, they left for Argentina's Patagonia region while I remained alone in Buenos Aires.

\*\*\*

Days turned into a week and still no money. Oh God, I wished it would arrive. One day, while sitting in a quiet Buenos Aires park under an ancient old Ombu tree writing poetry, I met a handsome, educated, young Argentinian man who spoke English. He recited some of his poetry to me. We talked for hours about poetry, literature, and the joys of life until very suddenly we were surrounded by three uniformed military policemen. They seemed to be very angry with him for talking to me and suspected him of doing something illegal. They checked my identification and searched my bag. They asked me if I had any drugs and then roughly took my friend away. I don't know what happened to this sweet man. I liked him very much. Considering what was happening in Argentina at the time, I strongly suspect that he became one of the thousands of "los desaparecidos" or "the disappeared" killed in the "Dirty War." I never heard from him again.

Now down to almost no money, it was becoming very apparent that it was not safe for me to be in Buenos Aires, especially alone. With the last of my cash, I bought a bus ticket to Montevideo, Uruguay. When my bus got close to the border, the bus driver told us in Spanish to go into the cafe for lunch and to return to the bus in thirty minutes. When we returned, my beautiful Bolivian poncho was missing. I had misunderstood what was happening. We were stopped because we were getting a different bus to cross into Uruguay and the old bus had departed with my handwoven poncho.

\*\*\*

My luck changed when I arrived in Montevideo. I met an American expat, Richard, who lived there with his Uruguayan wife. He was very kind and invited me to stay in their home. They taught me how to drink their national tea, Yerba Mate. A gourd was stuffed with Yerba Mate leaves and repeatedly filled with hot water as it was passed around in a circle like a joint with one metal straw for everyone to drink from. The first time the mate gourd was passed to me I politely said "Gracias" and was disappointed when it was never given to me again, but was passed to everyone else over and over. I later learned that in Uruguayan etiquette you only say thank you if you don't want any more mate.

As the mate gourd made it rounds, their conversation turned to what was a dangerous topic in Uruguay at the time—politics. I found out that there were estimated to be at least 6,000 political prisoners in Uruguayan prisons. Torture was believed to be widespread. The Uruguayan police and army torture methods included electric shocks on sensitive organs of the body and nearly drowning prisoners by submerging their heads in filthy water, a practice called "the submarine." The political prisoners were also psychologically tortured, denied water, prevented from sleeping, and injected with pentothal. It was made very clear to me that what I was hearing about that evening should not be repeated in Uruguay or my new friends' lives would be in danger for telling me.

Richard helped me arrange to have more money sent from my account in Canada to their Banco Commercial in Monteverde. Fortunately, this time my money arrived promptly. The money sent to Argentina never did arrive. It was

143

later discovered that it had been stolen by the National Bank of Argentina. Luckily for me, three months later the Bank of Nova Scotia in Canada that had been responsible for sending it, credited my account with the $500 that had been lost.

\*\*\*

With my new funds, I traveled north to visit the beautiful Iguazú Falls on the borders of Brazil, Paraguay, and Argentina.

I spent the night in an inexpensive hotel in Puerto Iguazú, on the Argentine side of the waterfalls, and in the morning went out for a big healthy breakfast at a posh hotel where I met a man, Ignacio, who told me all about the falls. He recounted tales of the local indigenous Guarani tribe and explained that in their language Iguazú meant "great waters." He said the falls were actually a group of many waterfalls spanning almost three kilometers, with some as high as 350 feet tall. They were made even more wondrous by the diverse tropical rainforest that surrounded them, making Iguazú Falls one of the most impressive natural wonders of the world. After eating a meal that would keep me going for most of the day, I excitedly set out to see the falls.

Iguazú Falls were even more breathtakingly magnificent than Ignacio had described. I took a small boat to an island at the base of the falls where I was surrounded by rushing rapids. It was a very hot day, so I enjoyed a natural shower under one of the smaller falls until I accidentally dropped my purse into the water. I watched my passport and all my money start to float away! Without thinking, I dove into the swirling waters to try to retrieve it. The rushing water at the base of the falls pushed me forward, throwing me against rocks that cut and bruised my legs, but I was successful. Eventually, I was able to climb out onto a rock ledge with my purse intact. I was delighted to find myself in a remarkable location that enabled me to climb in behind the roaring falls.

Sprinkled by a light mist, I leaned back against the black, wet rocks and became mesmerized by the incredibly powerful rushing cascade of water that passed before my eyes. I had entered a private, magical realm where I felt no distance between the physical and spiritual worlds. I recalled Igacio's story of how the Guarani tribe explained the creation of these magnificent waterfalls.

Each year the Guarani tribe sacrificed a young virgin to the Snake God, M'Boi who lived in the Iguazú River. One day a young woman named Napi walked by the river and the Snake God saw her reflection in the water. He thought she was the most beautiful woman he had ever seen and ordered her tribe to sacrifice her in the river for him. The elders feared and always obeyed the Snake God because he was the son of Tupa, the supreme God of all Gods.

The beautiful Napi was in love with a young man named Taruba. She wanted to marry him and did not want to be sacrificed to the Gods. However, the elders of her tribe ignored her desperate pleas and made plans to sacrifice her to the Snake God the day before she was to be wed.

Napi and Taruba decided to run away together. Unfortunately, the Snake God saw the young couple trying to escape in their canoe and followed them. When they realized the Snake God was behind them, they paddled as fast as they possibly could and managed to keep a few feet ahead of him. The Snake God became furious when he couldn't catch them and increased his slithering body size enormously to cause the Iguazú River to form new curves that dangerously rocked their little canoe. The lovers paddled on even harder keeping just ahead of him. Becoming more furious, the Snake God made the earth crack and split the rocks in the river which sent their canoe spinning. Taruba was thrown out onto the shore, while Napi was trapped inside the canoe. Just as she was about to smash into an embankment, the Snake God changed her into a huge rock, so she could never run away again. Taruba was horrified. He tried to rush down to help her, but the Snake God turned him into a palm tree. The malicious Snake God then created the enormous Iguazú Waterfalls to separate the couple forever and sank himself into the waters below the falls to keep an eye on them and make sure they could never touch each other again. Unable to truly unite, the lovers created a rainbow over Iguazú Falls which started at Taruba's palm tree in Brazil and reached over to Napi's rock in Argentina.

When I had been in the rushing waters below the falls, I felt the current start to pull me under when suddenly something strong had pushed me up to my rocky ledge of safety. Had the Snake God M'Boi helped me?

I spent half a day secretly hidden behind the magical falls and when I came out, I looked up and saw the lovers' beautiful rainbow bridge reaching over the falls. Suddenly, I longed to be with Sergio again. Part of me wanted to rush to Brazil to see him, but the adventurer in me was stronger.

*** 

The next day I crossed the border into Paraguay because, after all, it was close and I didn't know when I was going to be there

146

again. The first thing I noticed was how much poorer Paraguay appeared to be, compared to Argentina. The road was dusty and people still used donkeys for beasts of burden. The houses near the road were wooden shacks.

I met a Paraguayan man, Antonio, who spoke English quite well. He invited me to visit his farm nearby on the Parana River. He had a small sawmill near his house that he was using to turn the trees on his property into lumber. It appeared to me that he was destroying his entire forest by cutting down all of his trees. I expressed my concern and he explained that it didn't matter because in a few years his entire farm would be completely under water because the Itaipu Dam was being built upstream to generate electricity for Brazil and Paraguay. His plan was to harvest as many trees as he could before that happened.

Antonio hoped to make a fortune when the government bought his land to accommodate the massive flooding that would take place after the huge dam was finished. With that money, he and his wife, Carla, planned to go to Brazil to live. Carla was from Rio de Janeiro and she made it clear she absolutely hated living on this rustic farm in Paraguay. She missed the beach and city life. They did not have indoor plumbing and when I went to use their outhouse, I was horrified to see the latrine hole was swarming with huge masses of squirming white fly maggots. I could understand her unhappiness. After one night on their Paraguayan farm, I went back to Iguazú Falls and crossed the border into Brazil. As a bus carried me away from the magnificent waterfalls I wondered: what would the Snake God M'Boi think about his river being dammed up?

# Chapter 15
# Living in Brazil

## Carnaval

Black bodies shining

greased with sweat

reflecting in the night

an image

of the devil's soul,

Hot half-naked, retching

in the street.

I watch as time is lost,

lost civilization...

There are no controls

We are but screaming animals

who kill

who rape

who dance

who die!

With a feeling of great anticipation, I made my way to where Sergio lived with his parents in Santos, Brazil. I arrived at their home with a letter of introduction that Sergio had given to me in Buenos Aires before he left. I had been concerned that I might arrive at his parents' house not speaking any Portuguese and if he wasn't home at the time, I feared I was not going to be able to communicate with them. His letter described me as a "grande amiga." Initially, I took great offense because I thought "grande amiga" meant "fat friend." He had to explain that "grande" in this context meant a very good friend. We both laughed.

Sergio told me that his father had a coffee plantation, so I was expecting for him to live on a magnificent coffee estate. When I arrived at his home address in Santos, I was surprised to see a small two-bedroom house, with a little vegetable garden in front. I clapped my hands at the closed gate to find out where I had gone wrong. In Brazil when there is a closed gate in front of a house the appropriate etiquette is to clap instead of opening the gate and going up to the door and knocking. With a Pekingese dog barking at her side, a petite, gray-haired woman came out to greet me. She was Sergio's mother, Chica. She had been expecting me and welcomed me with open arms. *How could this be the right house? Where was the coffee plantation*? I wondered.

Sergio had told me that his father had a "plantado do couve," which sounded to me like a "plantation of coffee." As my Portuguese improved, I understood my error, "plantado do couve" meant his father had planted cabbage—not a plantation of coffee! There actually was cabbage growing in his father's front garden. It was impossible for me not to laugh at my own mistake. Yes, it is true that all relationships have communication misunderstandings at times, but when you don't speak the same language there are many more challenges to overcome.

When Sergio got home from work, he was happy to see me and invited me to stay with him and his family. It was lovely to be in a real home again. I was tired of staying in cheap hotels. The idea of staying in one place for a little while appealed to me, as did the opportunity to get to know Sergio's family.

\*\*\*

Early each morning before we were awake, Chica walked to the bakery so we could have warm, freshly baked bread for breakfast. She made us coffee by putting ground coffee beans into a pot of boiling water. The coffee was then filtered through a special cloth that looked like a dirty, old flannel sock. The sweet aroma of the strong coffee brewing was delightful. I had been disappointed that Sergio's father didn't have an expansive coffee plantation, but his mother made up for it with her delicious coffee.

Rice and beans were a part of every meal except breakfast. Chica taught me how to cook some Brazilian dishes, and we soon became great friends. She had grown up in a tiny, isolated fishing village on the coast north of Santos. She remembered that as a little girl they made their coffee not from water, but from sugar cane juice. No wonder she liked lots of sugar in her coffee. Each morning after breakfast she read every page of the newspaper, which was notably impressive because in the little village where she grew up, the only school available just went to grade three. She loved to read and keep up with current events.

In addition to maintaining the house, she worked from home to make her own money as a seamstress. Chica was very talented and spent hours making me a beautiful hand sewn, black sequined top to wear to a carnival party.

She made a point of telling me, "A woman should always have her own bank account and money."

Sergio's father, Pepe, worked as a metal lathe operator and coached a soccer team. After the weekend games he brought the entire soccer team's dirty uniforms home for his wife to wash—muddy socks and all. I was shocked by this. Chica was obliged to wash everything by hand because they didn't have a washing machine. She didn't seem to mind, but I did. Apparently, they previously had a maid, who did the washing, but she quit to move back home to Northern Brazil just before I arrived. I pushed for Pepe to buy his wife a washing machine and in time, he did.

Chica ironed everything that was hung out on the clothesline including panties, bras, socks, everything! I thought this was ridiculous, until she explained that clothes dried on the line often attracted tiny tropical insects and ironing killed them. That made perfect sense. We were after all, living in the tropics. I tried to help her out by doing some of the ironing, but when I melted Sergio's brother's nylon underwear with a too-hot iron, she sweetly told me that she preferred to do the ironing herself.

Sergio was working in telecommunications, and I soon found a job teaching both conversational and advanced English at the Brazil United States Cultural Center in Santos. I enjoyed teaching and approached it as if I was acting on the stage. With twenty students in my class ranging in age from fifteen to fifty, I had to be creative to keep their attention and get them to speak

English. At times I used a game of charades, at other times I became a clown, ridiculing myself. I did whatever it took to get my students engaged and soon became a very popular teacher.

The Santos University invited me to give a paid lecture on the differences between Canada and Brazil. I was very nervous because I was expected to speak for fifty minutes so I improvised and sang a few Canadian songs. Afterward someone asked for my autograph. This talk led to me to pick up a few private students who paid me $6 an hour to learn English. Life was good.

*Sergio and Alycin near Santos, Brazil.*

Sergio and I lived with his parents until we found our own one-bedroom apartment, with two balconies, for $100 a month on the beach, in the nearby town of Sao Vicente. Our cute little house was actually the top floor apartment of a house that was perched on the side of a mountain, bordered by wild tropical plants and colorful exotic flowers that grew on the steep cliffs surrounding it. The water in the house came from a fresh mountain stream. All the floors were made of red, ceramic tile which was very practical and easy to keep clean. Our kitchen had a white marble countertop which sounds quite opulent, but was actually common in most kitchens there at the time.

Before it got too hot in the mornings, we enjoyed a swim in the warm ocean and then stretched out on the beach to get some sun. Coastal Brazilians seemed to spend as much time relaxing on the beach and swimming as possible. I was happy to embrace this custom.

I loved living with Sergio by the seaside in Sao Vicente. After our morning swim, I often went to one of the farmers' markets, called ferias, that took place every day in different parts of the city where I purchased fresh pineapples, tangerines, papayas, and other seasonal fresh green vegetables for our meals. Most afternoons after work we went for a swim in the sea again. At night we walked along the beach with the moon and stars to light our way, listening to the gentle roar of the waves as a soft cool breeze blew in from the ocean.

In the small yard behind our house, I started a garden where I planted a few vegetables. They were growing well until our landlady who lived below us, chopped off a live chicken's head and sprayed the poor bird's spouting blood all over my garden. Horrified by her dramatic, frightening display, I abandoned my plants.

Later, I learned that our landlady was a spiritual leader deeply involved in Macumba/Candomblé's ancient customs. Macumba is an Afro-Brazilian religion that is a mixture of traditional African Religions, Roman Catholicism, and Brazilian Spiritualism. Its unusual, unique rituals are practiced by Brazilians from every walk of life as they worship a number of different Gods.

I strongly suspected our landlady had seen me bring home the flowers that I had innocently gathered on the beach. When Sergio learned that the flowers I had put in a vase in our house were found on the beach, he was initially appalled. Brazilians pay homage to Yemanja, the Goddess of the Sea, by placing flowers on the beach to be carried out with the next tide to her in the ocean. Unknowingly I had stolen the gifts intended for the Sea Goddess! I might as well have drunk holy water and snacked on stolen communion wafers. Sergio was amused by my blunder and forgave me, but our landlady never did.

Now whenever I walk by the sea, I feel the powerful presence of Yemanja in every wave. I believe she too forgave me. She has appeared to me twice, always when I was walking near water and in need of her energy. In my visions she has lustrous, long, black hair and wears a beautiful, light blue, full length gown that swirls gently around her body like the billowing waves of her ocean. Both times she smiled, looked directly at me and whispered as softly as a summer breeze, "Be strong and as free as the sea."

Yemanja kept me inspired.

Sergio and I were getting along great, really enjoying living together. We shared all of the cooking and household duties equally, except one. Our landlady wanted us to wash the private sidewalk in front of our house every day. I thought that was unnecessary and refused to do it, so Sergio did that job. Brazilians are incredible clean people. It is not unusual for them to take three showers a day, so I suppose washing the sidewalk was just another part of their clean culture.

In our evenings together Sergio and I discussed everything from Brazil's military dictatorship, to our future adventure travels. I was eager to travel again, explore more of South America and was saving my money to do it. My Portuguese was improving, but it was still not possible for me to carry on an in-depth conversation. Still, between my improving Portuguese and Sergio's broken English, we managed to communicate quite well most of the time.

We often met with his friends on the beach. Paulo, our former canoe-mate, had returned home from the Amazon to Santos before Sergio. He loved to take photos of their surfer friends as they rode on the crest of waves, while Sergio and I settled for body surfing in the warm, salty waters of incoming tides.

I was gradually adapting to Brazilian life. It took forever to get anything done. Life was much slower in Brazil than back in Canada. Very few people even had telephones. Sergio's parents didn't get a house phone until years later. To get anything done to you had to go in person. This didn't seem to bother the Brazilians. They had their own perception of time. "Live and wait."

Our former Canadian canoe-mates, Suzanne and Janice, returned to Santos after their travels in Argentina and Chile. Suzanne had come back to visit Paulo, and Janice soon fell in love with Paulo's cousin Nelio. Both of them decided to stay in

Santos, and, like me, found work teaching English. Suzanne, Paulo, Janice, and Nelio found a house to share with a wealthy, young American expat named Don. It was great to have them as neighbors. Their big house soon became the place we gathered to party.

Don was in the process of opening Santos's first ever fast food, fried chicken restaurant, *Restaurante Frango Frito de Santos Ltda*. Fast food was a new concept that had not really caught on in Brazil yet. I imagine that was because live-in maids were very inexpensive, so most people had maids to cook their meals, and those that didn't have a maid, could not afford to eat out.

My parents were decidedly curious about Sergio, so in a letter home I described him for them.

*Sergio is a kind, sensitive person, a bit shy at times but has a good sense of humor. He likes to travel as much as I do. His main interests are in the arts, especially photography. He has worked mostly with electronics to make a living. He would like to eventually support himself with artistic photography, but it is difficult to do, especially in Brazil. There will be an art exhibition here in Santos of his photography in July. He is eight months younger than me. We weigh the same sixty-four kilos. He has green eyes and brown hair with a reddish tint in the sun and a beard with a moustache (much like Elliott's). Being Brazilian he knows how to enjoy life. I am very fond of him.*

\*\*\*

I had been away from home for over a year when, with my encouragement, my mother bravely decided to visit me in Brazil. I think the real reason she came was to find out if I was

156

ever coming home and, of course, to meet the man I was living with. She flew down from Toronto, changed planes in Lima, Peru, and then flew across the Andes Mountains over Lake Titicaca to Rio de Janeiro. I took a bus to Rio and met her at the airport. It was wonderful to see her again.

After bartering with an airport taxi driver to get a good fare, we took his taxi to the Biarritz Hotel on Copacabana Beach. My talent at bartering has always helped me to travel on a shoestring budget. The hotel had a great location, was air conditioned, and fairly comfortable with a fridge stocked with beer, cold drinks, nuts, cookies, and small bottles of scotch. We helped ourselves and didn't discover until we checked out that the drinks in the fridge were not on the house. Still, the total bill for our entire stay of several days only came to $71.43. Copacabana's beautiful white beach was the widest beach my mother had ever seen. She loved it, and we had fun strolling along the beach from Copacabana to Ipanema singing, *The Girl from Ipanema*.

> *"Tall and tan and young and lovely*
> *The girl from Ipanema goes walking*
> *And when she passes*
> *Each one she passes goes, ahhhh…"*

Mom wanted to take in the sights of Rio so we went to the center of the city to change money, wandering into a few second-hand book shops on the way. Mom picked up a Brazilian copy of Grimm's Fairy Tales for my father. Dad was a collector and had an amazing collection of nearly 2000 antiquarian children's books in his home library. My childhood had been spent wandering into old bookshops with him as he looked for more children's books for his growing collection.

From there we visited the Museo do Indio (Indian Museum) and nearly lost our lives trying to get there crossing an auto bridge that did not have a sidewalk. We had to cling to the railings of the bridge to survive. Drivers in Rio were insane! They drove as fast as they possibly could and seemed to think the sight of a pedestrian on the street was a sign to speed up and head straight for them.

The objective of the Brazilian Indian Museum was to promote an accurate image of the indigenous cultures in an attempt to avoid common misconceptions and prejudices. Before the Portuguese arrived around 1500, Brazil had an indigenous population in the millions. As in North America, their numbers have now been radically reduced. Sorrowfully, logging, oil extraction projects, gold mines and even government-approved projects continue to diminish their territories and numbers. The exhibits were both fascinating and sad because many of the indigenous peoples represented there didn't exist anymore. I wondered how long the Dolphin Tribe I had visited would manage to survive.

We took a cable car up to the top of Rio's famous solid granite Sugarloaf Mountain where a pair of two-foot-long Tegu lizards sunned themselves next to us as we enjoyed the magnificent view of the beautiful city of Rio de Janeiro. Mom was impressed by the big lizards, so later that day we went to the National Museum (Brazil's oldest scientific institution) and the Zoo. The Rio de Janeiro Zoological Park had a variety of animals, including many gorgeous Amazonian parrots and brilliantly colored beaky toucans. Both of us found it depressing to see all of these impressive, intelligent birds that were meant to fly free, kept in cages. I have never understood why people want to imprison and control wild animals.

From Rio we took a train that passed through several small villages, lush tropical forests, and cultivated farmland. As the train approached the big metropolis of Sao Paulo, we were disturbed to see the large, dirty industrial areas that surround it. From Sao Paulo we took a bus on a new four-lane highway to Sao Vicente where Sergio met us at the bus station.

Mom whispered to me, "Sergio looks a bit like one would imagine the original Portuguese adventurers looked when they arrived in Brazil centuries ago."

*Did she see what I saw in him? My fearless, brave Brazilian hero ready for the new adventures we would share together.*

After Mom settled in, I took her by bus to Gonzaga, an attractive shopping area in Santos. Sao Vicente and Santos were so close together, it was hard to tell where one town started and the other ended. We window shopped and were shocked at some of the prices. One simple cotton dress in a window was 900 cruzeiros which back then was about $90. Mom was appalled at how much food cost, even in the local farmers' markets.

She exclaimed, "The prices are as high or higher than in Canada!"

With the average monthly wage in Brazil at the time being only $75 a month, we both wondered how the ordinary Brazilian could manage to survive.

Sergio's parents had us all over for a delicious dinner of Brazilian roast pork at their house. After we ate, we watched a Novella on their color television. Novellas (Soap Operas) in Brazil at that time were incredibly popular. During the evening hours when the Novella was on TV, the streets of the residential neighborhoods were empty because everyone was inside watching. Sergio and I didn't have a television so this was Mom's first time to watch TV in Brazil. Not speaking any Portuguese, she didn't understand anything of what was being said, but she did notice that the soap opera was interspersed with many commercials and much government propaganda.

I wanted to show Mom one of the places I loved near Santos, so we took a ferry to Guaruja and then traveled by bus to my favorite, yet to be discovered by tourists, Pernambuco beach. After swimming in the sea, Sergio led us up a path to a rocky cliff where we could wander through the uninhabited rainforest above the beach.

Suddenly he shouted, "Cobra! Cobra!"

Mom was terrified and screamed expecting to see a giant King Cobra coiled and ready to strike in front of us. Mom did not know that "cobra" was the word for snake in Brazil. Sergio had seen a harmless grass snake on the trail ahead of us, and he didn't want her to miss seeing the little green beauty. After she calmed down and understood her mistake, even she was amused.

It was hard for Mom to get to know Sergio well because he spoke very little English. They both tried, but it was an insurmountable challenge. Conversation was impossible without me doing the translation. It was frustrating for all of us.

That night we went out to dinner in a fancy pizza restaurant in Santos. Pizza was brought to Brazil by Italian immigrants in the late 1880s and was extremely popular. Along with the traditional toppings I was used to, the creative Brazilians included hearts of palm, fresh corn, mashed potatoes, grilled sausages, potato sticks, and even curried chicken with coconut milk. Nothing was off the table when it came to pizza toppings in Brazil. The aroma of melting cheese filled the air as our charming waiter in his pristine white jacket served us our delicious pizza. I had to quickly let my mother know that unlike in Canada, pizza in Brazil was always eaten with a knife and fork. Eating pizza with your hands in Brazil was considered quite gauche. Learning new customs was one of the things I enjoyed most about traveling—no matter how strange or different they may have seemed.

\*\*\*

The following night Sergio's parents invited us to their club for a Samba celebration. It was a sort of mini Brazilian Carnival that did not even start until 11:00 p.m. Brazilians love to party at any time day or night. We sat at a round table, covered with a white table cloth, drinking caipirinhas made with crushed lime, sugar, and Brazilian cachaça. As the lively Samba band's steady rhythm cut across the room, the stirring beat made it impossible to not get up and gyrate across the dance floor. The music transported me to the magical soul of Brazil as we swayed to the lively beat of the Samba band until 4:00 a.m. It was great fun. Everyone danced. We all had a wonderful night.

By the time we got home it was almost daybreak. Before going to bed, we walked down to our beach to watch the sun rise. As the early morning golden rays of light rose above where the ocean met the sky, I danced in the sand and placed flowers in the waves for Yemanja, the Goddess of the Sea.

# Chapter 16
# Bolivia by Train

*Old fashioned lady*
*child of your dreams*
*listen to the children*
*cry themselves to sleep*

*Old fashioned lady*
*The sky it's still blue*
*Springtime brings flowers*
*they're meant for you*

*Rest quietly now child*
*while the moon*
*reigns the sky,*
*Tomorrow brings sunshine*
*tomorrow is nigh-*

*Follow the rainbows*
*reach for the sky*
*Live every moment,*
*All it takes is to try.*

As much as I enjoyed living with Sergio on the beach, it didn't really feel like home. I was getting tired of staying in one place.

I missed traveling and wanted to see more of South America, so when it was time for my mother to head back to Lima to catch her flight home, I suggested we travel overland to Peru together. She loved my proposal, but had no idea what she was getting herself into, traveling with me. We packed our bags and got ready to leave.

I kissed Sergio goodbye at the bus station. It felt strange saying goodbye to him, because I didn't know when or if I was ever going to see him again. It was even more difficult for him, because he was being left behind, whereas I was excited to be traveling again on a new adventure. Even if Sergio could get away from work to travel with us it was going to cost him over a thousand dollars for a Brazilian exit visa.

This was the first time my mother and I ever traveled together. Yes, we had traveled as a family, with my father and little brother, but this was the first and only time just the two of us ever got to travel together. It was a priceless once-in-a-lifetime experience where we got to know each other better in new ways every day.

We started out by taking a bus to Sao Paulo where we caught a train for $12 each (138 cruzeiros) to Corumba, which was on the border of Brazil and Bolivia. We traveled first-class on this train. It was very comfortable and had a lovely dining car that Mom and I both enjoyed. Our train passed through small towns where most houses had small vegetable gardens, over rolling hills, across huge ranches and through the middle of banana plantations with green fruit not quite close enough to reach.

In Bauru, Brazil, we had to change trains but were not able to get a sleeping compartment which was disappointing, especially for Mom. I didn't mind, but Mom was hot, exhausted, and just wanted to have a bed to sleep in for the long night. The thought of sitting up all night was not appealing to her. Finally, at 8:30 p.m., I managed to get us a sleeping compartment for $13 (150 cruzeiros) for the night. Fortunately, our bed compartment was very comfortable with a fan to cool us off. The dining car on this train was very disappointing, offering us only stale, dry sandwiches.

*** 

The next day our view out the window became more interesting as we traveled through a rainforest that grew more and more dense, only occasionally interspersed by small indigenous villages. Wild Rhea birds raced past us as the many other exotic water birds including elegant black and white Jabiru storks looked on.

Eventually we arrived in Corumba, Brazil, at 9:00 p.m. after thirty-eight hours on trains. Exhausted, we walked across a field with our luggage to a hotel that could be seen from the train station. It was filthy, with huge cockroaches crawling on the walls, sad-looking cots for beds, and an untold number of strange tropical insects flying all over the room. Mom refused to stay there, even for one night, so we trudged back across the field with our luggage where I found a taxi at the train station and asked him to take us to a decent hotel. He took us to Corumba's Grande Hotel. It may have been grand at one time, but was rather run down now. Still, it was clean so we got a suite with a bathroom and two fans, one in each bedroom. After our long train ride, it was wonderful to be able to shower and get clean again. I washed out a few clothes while Mom went down to the lobby with her Portuguese/English dictionary and managed to buy us some beer and bottled water to take back to our room. Exhausted, we collapsed into bed and fell soundly asleep.

Mom was having a hard time adjusting to the extremely hot tropical heat. It was so humid that we constantly perspired and stayed perpetually drenched in sweat. Drinking enough water to stay hydrated in these conditions was difficult especially when the only safe drinking water was bottled water.

*** 

It was already hot when we arose at 5:30 the next morning. Mom dressed appropriately wearing a cool summer dress, flip flops, and a straw hat. Our hotel breakfast came with coffee, fresh bread, and marmalade. They called it marmalada but it was not like any marmalade I had ever tasted. It was more like guava jam. Mom always drank black coffee in the morning without sugar, so it was an adjustment for her to start her day with the hotel coffee that came already loaded with lots of sugar. Due to the intense humid heat, the people in this town went to work at 6:00 a.m. so we also set out early to get our visas. We had no trouble getting our exit visas stamped in our passports by the Brazilian officials.

Next, we went to the Bolivian consulate to get our visas for Bolivia. The uniformed Bolivian official was very charming, but shook his head solemnly after looking at our passports.

He looked me straight in the eye and announced, "I am very sorry but the Bolivian border has been closed to all

Canadians because Bolivia has broken off relations with Canada."

We were shocked. Mom and I looked at each other in horror. *What should we do?* I suddenly remembered reading in the news that a Canadian Union Official had been put under house arrest in La Paz, Bolivia. *This must have started the breakdown in relations.* We stood speechless looking at him almost in tears as his serious expression slowly changed into a hearty laugh. We realized that he was just teasing us. This was his idea of a joke. He roared with laughter. We laughed with relief. Still chuckling, he stamped Bolivian visas into our passports.

We tried to exchange some US dollars into Bolivian pesos only to discover this was not possible to do in Corumba, so we checked out of our hotel and took the 9:00 a.m. bus across the border to Puerto Suarez, Bolivia. The road to Puerto Suarez was unbelievably bumpy.

Mom exclaimed, "I don't know how any cars survive on these roads!"

The road was so rough the bus could not travel more than twenty miles an hour for the entire trip. Additionally, the bus driver had to continuously honk his horn to get goats, cattle, and pigs off the roadway so we could pass. The heat continued to increase as we reached the hamlet of Puerto Suarez. Mud stucco houses surrounded a pleasant square with a fountain in the middle. The bus driver let us off at the only "air conditioned" hotel—Hotel Bamby which was 160 Bolivian pesos ($8) a night. It turned out that "air conditioned" meant there was a fan in the room. In this oppressive heat a fan actually did make a difference. Our room also had a shower and a toilet that flushed when you pulled a string to let the water out of the tank above the toilet.

\*\*\*

We booked passage on the plane that was scheduled to leave at 11:00 a.m. the following morning and set out to find the local magistrate to get our passports officially stamped for entry into Bolivia. This magistrate was quite a character—very old, in his eighties no doubt, with white hair, and only one tooth showing in his mouth. We found him sitting in front of his office shirtless under a shady tree. He invited us into his dirty office which was also his impoverished home where he insisted upon going into a back room to put on a shirt before doing official business with us. When he returned, he took out an old plastic bag full of various stamps and proceeded to stamp our entry into our passports in a very polite and official manner.

We entertained ourselves by sitting in the town square for a while but the afternoon heat was so intense that we returned to our hotel room and collapsed until suppertime. For dinner we went to a place that served a tasty spicy pasta dish, but before we could finish our meal, we were attacked by masses of aggressive mosquitoes so we hurriedly returned to our hotel room. That night a heavy rain lulled us to sleep.

\*\*\*

The next morning at the very early hour of 5:00 a.m., we were awakened by a rooster crowing outside our window—followed by machine gun fire! Terrified, we looked out our window to see an army battalion shooting at the building behind our hotel. *Oh my God! Had a revolution started?* I checked with the hotel clerk and she assured me that the army was just holding firing practice. This was followed by band practice. There was no point trying to go back to sleep so I went to the local bakery and bought us some rolls to eat in the plaza for breakfast. The rolls tasted like salty, dry rocks. They were completely inedible. After attempting a few bites, we gave the rest of our rolls to the three street dogs that had shyly followed me from the bakery.

We returned to our hotel to check out and get a taxi to the airport when the hotel receptionist told us our plane was not going to arrive today because the dirt landing strip was too muddy for a plane to land after the tremendous rain storm we had had during the night. She cheerily explained the next plane should arrive a week from today if it didn't rain again. Neither of us wanted to spend a week in Puerto Suarez. When she saw our disappointment, she suggested that we could take the train instead, which sounded like a reasonable alternative.

The next train was leaving in less than an hour for Santa Cruz so I rushed into the town square to find a taxi to take us to the train station. The only taxi I could find was a beat-up old jeep pickup truck which for fifty cents agreed to take us to the train station. Mom and I jumped into the back of the truck with our luggage and I asked the driver to hurry. The driver smiled and nodded, but still stopped several times to pick up three more men who crowded into the back of the pickup with us. The road to the station was worse than the road we had taken to get to Puerto Suarez. It was full of splashing mud holes and big rocks that the driver tried to dodge by suddenly swerving one way then the other, jolting us back and forth in the process.

By the time we got to the station the train had already arrived. The entrance was surrounded by a massive mud hole with pigs wallowing in it. Dogs, chickens, goats, and a mob of people were all milling around us trying to get to the small two-car train.

Mom got her foot stuck in the mud trying to maneuver her big suitcase, straw hat, and bulky purse toward the train. She was wearing flip flops and one broke in the sucking mud. Ultimately, she was forced to take off her broken sandal so she could pull herself out of the mud, all the while curious grunting pigs and barking dogs swarmed around her. The rest of the people at the station nonchalantly watched her frustrating struggle.

Fearing we were not going to make the train, I rushed ahead as she continued to struggle in the mud shouting back at her, "Hurry up, Mom, or we'll miss the train!"

Finally, a kind man pulled her suitcase out of the muck, enabling her to at long last limp her way to the platform, with one sandal on and one muddy broken flip-flop in her hand.

I raced into the station to buy us two first-class tickets, but they were completely sold out. In fact, there were no tickets left for the train at all! Mom was desperate. She did not want to spend another night in this sweltering mud hole of a town. As a cloud of hungry mosquitoes attacked her, she crossed her fingers, closed her eyes and started to pray for a way out of Puerto Suarez. Just before the train departed, her prayers were answered. I managed to buy us second-class tickets for $10 each from two men who had watched us arrive. This was more than twice the original price of the tickets, but at least we could get on the train. Mom would have paid anything. The next train wasn't due until Saturday and this was Wednesday.

As I checked our bags, Mom waited on the platform. While she waited, an efficacious policeman pointed a machine gun at her and started questioning her. All she could say in Spanish to the aggressive officer was, "No hablo Espanol, No habla Espanol."

I suppose she did look rather suspicious, standing there covered in mud, with only one shoe.

He insisted she hand over her passport shouting, "Passaporte! Passaporte!"

That she understood and handed him her passport which he checked over very slowly and finally returned to her so we could get on the train. Our seats for the long twelve-hour train ride to Santa Cruz were hard straight-backed wooden benches that we shared with chickens and indigenous Bolivians who were all traveling with big cloth-wrapped bundles full of untold treasures. Our car was completely packed with men, women, children, and crying babies. By all appearances our miscellaneous train companions were extremely poor. They were also wonderfully friendly and welcomed us with big smiles.

Once the train left Puerto Suarez, we passed through beautiful areas of dense rainforest. Every so often the train came to a small village with adobe mud houses and thatched roofs where the engineer repeatedly blew the train's whistle to shoo the many wandering pigs, goats, Brahman cattle, and dogs off the tracks. At every village we came to, the train stopped and old women and children ran up to our window selling all kinds of food—cooked meals, fried pies, legs of pork, mangos by the bag, apricots, and other curious fruits we could not identify.

At one stop we were offered an armadillo baked in the shell. We passed on that! One woman on our train gave Mom a big ripe mango.

Mom genuinely appreciated it and thanked the woman as best she could with a mixture of English and Spanish, "Gracias, best mango I ever tasted. Absolutely delicious."

*Children selling food to Alycin and her mother*
*on the train to Santa Cruz, Bolivia.*

Our train stopped in a densely forested area in the middle of nowhere. I looked out our open window, and just before our train started up again, I saw the tail end of a huge snake pass into the rainforest in front of the train. I didn't tell Mom. She had already had a traumatic enough day.

My friend Kandy, years later, had a similar experience on the same Bolivian train route. Her train was forced to stop to let an enormous Anaconda snake pass over the tracks to prevent the giant reptile from derailing the train. Although her story sounded outrageous at the time, I didn't doubt her. It left me even more convinced that the Snake God M'Boi was real and living in this rainforest.

Many hours later we finally arrived in Santa Cruz. Mom's feet were sore and her back was killing her. She told me to tell the taxi driver that picked us up at the train station to take us to the Santa Cruz Holiday Inn.

The cab driver shook his head and stated, "No, Holiday Inn, Muy caro! Muy caro!"

I explained to her that the taxi driver said the Holiday Inn was too expensive.

Mom indignantly replied, "I don't care how much it costs! Tell him to take us there."

My poor exhausted mother, covered in dried, filthy pig mud, with only one sandal on looked quite pitiful demanding to be taken to the Holiday Inn. She had been such a good sport during these challenging circumstances. I implored him to take us there, but the cab driver was insistent. He refused and took us instead to the surprisingly pleasant, clean Roma Hotel that was just $10 a night for a double room. We later learned that the Santa Cruz Holiday Inn was the most expensive Holiday Inn anywhere in the world, because it was where the wealthy

Bolivian drug lords stayed. Our cabbie may have done us a favor.

*** 

From Santa Cruz we flew with Lloyd Aereo Boliviano Airlines to Cochabamba on a very agreeable thirty-minute flight that cost only $15 each and covered the same distance that our arduous twelve-hour second-class train ride had taken. In this fertile valley surrounded by the Andes Mountains the weather was now delightfully cooler and very pleasant. We found a great place to stay. The Cochabamba Gran Hotel had extensive beautiful tropical gardens with a swimming pool, tennis courts, fountains, rose bushes, and flowering trees. Our $10 a night double room even had a bathtub which was very unusual in South America. Every other bathroom I had been in since I had left home only had a shower. I enjoyed a long soak in the tub. It was my first bath in over a year!

In the evenings Mom and I went down to the hotel bar for drinks and played Yahtzee which both amused and entertained the Bolivian men in the bar. No other women were ever in the bar. The men were quite impressed that we entered their bar without a male escort, drank alcohol, and played with dice, which to them probably looked like gambling. We caused quite a sensation.

I fell in love with Cochabamba's big friendly street dogs. These beautiful, healthy canines with long, curly hair roamed freely throughout the city. I wanted to take one home with me, but Mom wisely talked me out of it. These guardian hounds of the city could be heard barking in the distance at night which made me feel secure.

Indigenous saleswomen in Cochabamba's artisan market wore impressive tall white top hats, voluminous skirts, and colorful woolen shawls as they displayed their wares. Mom purchased a few warm alpaca sweaters to bring home as gifts and from Cochabamba we flew to the world's highest national capital: La Paz, Bolivia.

# Chapter 17

# Inca Mysteries in Peru

La Paz, Bolivia, is 11,942 feet above sea level, nestled in a sweeping high plateau in the midst of the Andes Mountains. We paced ourselves when we arrived because the high mountain air was noticeably thinner so it took us a few days to get used to the lack of oxygen.

Returning to this old Inca city felt like a full circle prophecy coming true, for La Paz was where I had been guided through my maternal genetic ancestry by the mystical hallucinogenic cactus, San Pedro. It was where I had learned to believe in the magic of my imagination. And here I was again, this time with my mother, creating new pages in our family's life history. This mystical cactus had played a central role in the heart of the pre-Colombian Chavin culture's elaborate religious rituals that were considered to be precursors of the Inca Empire. In fact, San Pedro is thought to be what inspired the complex Inca civilization to develop in the first place. *I could feel the visions of San Pedro still guiding me.*

From La Paz we traveled to the highest navigable lake in the world, Lake Titicaca. It was formed 60 million years ago when a colossal earthquake cracked the Andes Mountains in half and created a crater which filled with water from melting glaciers. Lake Titicaca was the birthplace of the Inca's Sun God where all life began and is often referred to as the cradle of the world. The Island of the Sun is the largest island in the lake and home to many Incan ruins.

The most fascinating thing we found on the clear blue green waters of Lake Titicaca were the man-made floating islands that had been built centuries before by the innovative Uru people. These moveable islands were made from the same reed materials as their beautiful handmade reed boats that they still use to navigate the lake. The clever Uru tribe originally made their floating islands to live on to escape the aggressive Incas who forced them off their homeland on the shores of Lake Titicaca.

*Bolivian farmer bringing in his harvest near Lake Titicaca.*

Next, we headed to the Imperial city of Cusco, Peru where we stayed in the heart of what had been the largest empire in Pre-Columbian America, the Incan empire. Leonard's Lodging, a $4 a night guest house was charmingly located in the middle of the city just a twenty-minute walk from the Plaza de Armas which had been the original starting point of what became the capital city of the Incan Empire. We were surrounded by the surviving 3000-year-old Incan buildings made from stones so precisely cut and shaped that they fit together without any mortar. To our delight over breakfast, the owner of our guest house, William Leonard, a retired American, happily shared his knowledge of the Incas, as well as the aliens who had mated with them. Aliens from outer space interbreeding with humans was how he explained the Incas' remarkable accomplishments in architecture. Leonard had come to Peru years before with terminal cancer and claimed to have been completely cured in Cusco by herbs and hot peppers. His local Peruvian wife, Luisa, made beautiful traditional hand knit dolls, two of which we purchased to take home as gifts.

*Alycin met children hiking on the Inca Trail*
*near Cusco, Peru.*

Wandering around Cusco, it was impossible to ignore the poverty, with women and children begging on street corners. One evening an obviously hungry little boy approached us asking for money. We were about to enter a restaurant so we invited him to join us for dinner. We ordered the meal of the day for each of us. He ate his food in the restaurant very politely, but absolutely refused to eat his spinach. I guess kids are the same everywhere.

Mom developed a fever and bad cough that was working its way into her lungs. Very concerned about her, I asked Luisa where I might find a pharmacy with medicine for my mother. She assuredly gave me a name and directions to what turned out to be the Witch's Market. I wandered through the market, passing people selling clay pots, baskets, herbs, handmade charms and, strange-looking amulets until I finally found her suggested pharmacist. She was an old, bent over indigenous woman who did look exactly like my image of a witch. Dressed in rags, she sat cross legged on the street with her back to an ancient Incan stone wall. Lined up in front of her were dozens of cloth bags full of herbs and other odd things like dried frogs and bats.

In my best Spanish I asked her for medicine for my mother's cough and fever, "Mama tos y fiebre. Necesito medicina."

Slowly she considered my request, perhaps judging my sincerity, then recognizing the concern in my eyes, nodded and began to put together an assortment of her herbs into a small cloth bag.

"Haz que tu madre beba este té esta noche." (Make your mother drink this tea tonight.)

I thanked her, paid her for the bag of medicinal herbal tea and returned to my mother who was getting worse. I was not sure if I should trust the old woman's medicine, but I had nothing else to give her, so as directed by the witch, I made Mom drink the tea. She drank a full cup of it and fell soundly asleep. I too fell asleep hoping I had not just poisoned my mother.

To my great relief, Mom woke up the next morning feeling miraculously well. Both her cough and fever were completely gone, and she was eager for us to hike up to Machu Picchu! So, we did.

*JoAnn Hayes, the author's mother, hiking at Machu Picchu.*

More than 7,000 feet above sea level, tucked high up in the Andes Mountains, one of the new seven wonders of the world, Machu Picchu rests remarkably on a mountain top. With over 100 flights of stone stairs and 150 buildings all made of large perfectly carved rocks it truly is a remarkable work of man. It is believed the Incas didn't use wheels to move any of the multitude of heavy rocks up the mountain either. They rolled and pushed them. *Were they inspired by San Pedro or as Leonard had suggested: by mating with aliens?*

*Alycin at Machu Picchu.*

It was not easy hiking at this altitude, but we wanted to explore as much as we possibly could. We stopped for a rest in what had been an old temple when we were passed by an elderly American woman with blue-gray hair who didn't seem to be the least bit fazed by the altitude.

I asked her, "How can you hike so quickly here? We are out of breath."

She smiled and replied confidently, "I chew coca leaves."

Then she proceeded to pull a few dried leaves out of her bag to show us. She went on to explain, "I love how they give me energy. I always fill my pockets with coca leaves when I fly home to the States."

Coca leaves or any form of cocaine are completely illegal in the United States. I suppose the American border guards didn't suspect this sweet old lady of smuggling drugs. I don't think she even realized they were illegal, which made her the perfect drug mule. Her permed blue head quickly bobbed on ahead out of sight. No doubt, coca leaves must have been a contributing factor in helping to build Machu Picchu too.

*Machu Picchu, Peru.*

We returned to Cusco and flew to Lima, Peru, where Mom needed to catch her flight home. We stayed at Senora Sumanez's lovely guest house in Miraflores, a suburb of Lima. It was a pretty place with a floral garden and within walking distance of the Pacific Ocean.

Strolling along the seaside gave me time to think. I was starting to miss Sergio. My plan was to see my mother off at the airport in Lima and continue on to Ecuador and the Galapagos Islands for Christmas by myself, but I wasn't ready to tell Mom goodbye. We'd had such a wonderful time traveling together, and I missed my dad and brother, Elliott, so I changed my mind at the last minute and flew home to Canada with her.

\*\*\*

As our plane took off, we soared high over the majestic white peaks of the Andes Mountains, followed by the Amazon rainforest. From the sky the winding rivers in the Amazon Basin looked like giant snakes twisting and turning their way through a vast tropical forest. I had spent months navigating these rivers, enduring exhausting hardships and meeting face to face with dangerous challenges. Had I been guided and magically protected by M'Boi the Snake God? Anything and everything is possible in the Amazon!

By following my dreams, I had discovered not only new parts of the planet, but also new parts of myself. I had learned that I could be as strong as I dared to be.

Our plane pushed up higher through enormous white billowing clouds and my mind floated ahead to dreams of future travels, in faraway undiscovered lands.

The adventure never ends;
the trail simply changes.

# Epilogue

Over time I lost track of most of the people I met traveling.

The last I heard from my Costa Rican friend, Clemencia, was in 1977 when she sent me a postcard.

French Canoe buddy, Christian called at my parents' house in Canada in 1978, while I was studying at the University of Texas in Austin. He told them he was going to visit me in Texas, but I never heard from him after that.

Paulo stayed in Brazil and became a professional photographer in Sao Paulo.

Janice married Paulo's cousin Nelio and they moved to Victoria, Canada.

Years later Suzanne drove across Canada to visit me with her youngest daughter. Recently she walked the Camino Trail in Spain.

Sergio and I got married at my parents' house in Stratford, Ontario, Canada, four years after we met on the bus in Colombia. A few years later, I gave birth to our wonderful son, Adrian, in Vancouver, British Columbia, Canada. My marriage to Sergio lasted for almost ten years. A major bone of contention was that he didn't want to travel anymore. After we divorced, I started adventure traveling again, often with my son, but that's another story.

Made in USA - North Chelmsford, MA
1306989_9780973032048
02.28.2022 1609